Street Politics:
It Ain't Your Daddy's GOP Anymore!

Matt Jordan

DEDICATION

To Lyn, for understanding, spoiling,
focusing, helping, tolerating, caring for
and loving me.

CONTENTS

ACKNOWLEDGMENTS

Much of the gratitude for making this book possible would have to go to my wife Lynette. She has an amazing capacity for patience where I am concerned, especially when I am in the "project zone". I tend to obsess and exhibit a mercurial temper. She takes it all in stride. She was also a real trooper sitting next to me for hours, proof reading and offering invaluable insight.

Thanks also go to my son Phil, network genius, for being there at the eleventh hour when it looked like the wheels were coming off the wagon. When it comes to the operation of these confounded google machines, I am still in diapers.

PREFACE

10 August 2016

Last year I sat down to finally lay out a message that had been burning inside me since Bush 41 yawned his way through his failed reelection campaign. I wanted to demonstrate how a new approach was needed to bring repeatable success to conservative politics.

As I finished the first draft, the present campaign was starting to gel. I used some examples of what I was seeing in those early days in my final draft. I was hoping to get the attention of the candidates. I was confident enough in my assessments to say the information herein was valuable. I was also imploring you, the voter, to make demands of the candidates.

It is bittersweet looking back over fourteen months and seeing what went well and what didn't. While I can draw real satisfaction in the accuracy of my predictions, certain disappointments are brought into relief.

As of this writing, there are 90 days left before Election Day. Donald Trump and Hillary Clinton are locked in a most disgraceful competition for mediocrity. Trump shows no signs of letting go of his schoolgirl Twitter antics, and still can't express a complete thought without reading it. Clinton is piling lie upon lie, in every aspect of her campaign, and when speaking of her illegal server specifically. Both are appealing to the lowest motives of the voter. Both have written us off as stupid. The press is circling, preparing to slice Trump to ribbons, all as I predicted in this book and at *streetpolitics.us*.

Also, as predicted on the website, the FBI and the "Justice" Department have allowed themselves to be used as goons to further Democrat ambitions.

A Sad I-Told-You-So From Me.

As things got rolling last year, I warned of all of this. I also spelled out what a candidate needed to do in order to win. All of my warnings and predictions have been vindicated in the ensuing fourteen months. Sadly, much of the vindication has resulted in the mess we have now.

On the Republican side, Trump proved all my conclusions from the first two chapters of this book. Sadly, he wouldn't have understood the third chapter (Conservative) if he read it, and he made a mockery of my points on fratricide. There were still all the points in seventeen other chapters that he could have, but never did employ with any success. He is to be forgiven in that he can't form sentences.

Ironically, the one who proved this book to be an invaluable tool for modern politicians was Bernie Sanders. With the exception of the Second Amendment, there is not a thing he and I would agree on politically. I would never vote for him in a general election.

BUT!. . . Bernie went from near-zero name recognition to a man the Democrats had to throw under a bus in order to beat. The entire machine was put to work to keep BJ Bill's wife ahead of the game. He caused Clinton to go all-out, loony socialist and she still had to fight all the way to California to beat him. Debates were rigged to marginalize Sanders and the other Democrat candidates. "Super delegates" were bought and paid for in numbers that would be insurmountable, using an honest democratic process.

And how did Sanders hold on so long and do so well? He was himself! He wasn't risk-averse (most of the time - he did let the felon off the hook on the server thing way too early). He wasn't afraid to get loud and "touch noses", as I like to say. He had a clear message. He defined it well. When it was required, he was teaching. He dealt with real issues – stupidly perhaps if

MATT JORDAN

you have a job and know that Socialism is a failed system – one after another, along the lines I encouraged Republicans to do. In other words, he followed all the principals in this book, if not the policy direction, to explode onto the scene and grow his influence.

As a result of their blunt messages and rejection of political "orthodoxy" both men bulldozed nearly all the pundits. The talking heads that weren't surprised were the ones who sold out and jumped on one of the political bandwagons early. And then there was little, freethinking me. If the situation we are facing now were not so dire, I'd enjoy a loud, giggly "neener, neener" moment. But it is dire.

And it isn't for lack of trying. I did my best to promote my book. I even sent copies to a few campaigns. I told them if they would just be themselves and get loud, they could use some of my ideas without citation. No one took me up on it.

Ah well, I'm an unknown entity. Maybe they'll listen from here on out. The idea **is** to create conservative victory for years into the future. So now I write for the future. This work is just a primer. It is intended to give you a specifically political look at the conservative movement. I've kept my delivery brash and light intentionally, *even in the end notes.* I've endeavored to be practical and pragmatic. I will follow this later with a book on how the proper approach to conservatism and citizenship can be brought into this century and improve the way we function and relate as a society.

And so we begin our argument. Let's roll back time by fourteen months...

FORWARD

"Politicians and diapers should be changed frequently, and for the same reason. "
- Eca De Queiros

Just prior to his launch into near space and the history books, Alan Shepard had a hot mike moment for the ages. In what is now known as Alan Shepard's prayer America's first Astronaut was heard to say, "Don't fuck up, Shepard..."

It seems the modern Republican must murmur a similar prayer every day. Before facing the press or giving a speech, some of the GOP's most powerful leaders must look in the mirror and say, "Just let me get through this news cycle without saying anything too controversial. "

In an effort to avoid controversy, Republicans come across as afraid of their own message, or worse, having no message. There are exceptions, of course. What would a day be like without Lindsay Graham calling for troops to be sent to Syria, Iraq, Libya, or wherever else people are behaving badly. And who doesn't love watching Chris Christie carry his bulk into an audience to touch noses with an Occupy Sissy Street type and leave the guy whimpering and looking at his shoes. There will be exceptions to all my characterizations in this book.

But as a political party, we seem to think the road to Capital Hill or the White House is paved with fluffy rhetorical pillows where the winner is the one who didn't take too strong a stand on things. Those who set themselves apart with clean, sharp positions are the exception to the rule. And this, dear reader, is the reason Republicans do not utterly dominate the governing class today. Well, that and the absence of a paper ballot, early voting and voter fraud. It goes without saying this phenomenon *is* institutionalized. Let a Republican suffer a moment of honesty and make a comment that isn't from the official book of progressive correctness, then watch the party implode. In distancing themselves from the offender, most of the big-name hacks will turn squarely away from their own principals, hoping the press might give them a personal pass and not ask them directly what they think. The Dems tend to do the exact opposite on their end, especially when the Democratic comments in question are, as is often the case, outright lies. We will see more on this in the chapters on *Growing a Pair* and *Message.*

It is my hope someone with an ounce of personal courage can take advantage of the opportunity on offer in this election year. The timing cannot be better for the GOP. The nation now knows, beyond a doubt the President is not only a spineless orator, completely out of his depth, but is also an undeservedly self-absorbed fop. They are coming to realize what a complete skank Harry Reid was in his tenure (such knowledge came as a side benefit of McConnell playing nice and making it too easy for Dems to run *his* Senate). Nancy Pelosi is now seen as an embarrassment, nothing more. Hilary has hundreds of hours of video available to anyone wishing to use it, demonstrating how utterly dishonest and wrong-headed she is on damn near everything.

So, Conservatives, do you want to win this **and future elections**? Do you want to win in a landslide? Do you? *Do you, really?* Then park your egos and pay attention. There are things those empty suits you surround yourself with are not letting you do. They handle you this way at your peril.

Making it Stick!

Once, when taken to task for his rough language, George Patton responded, "When I want my men to remember something important, to really make it stick, I give it to them double dirty. It may not sound nice to a bunch of little old ladies, at an afternoon tea party, but it helps my soldiers to remember. You can't run an army without profanity, and it has to be eloquent profanity. An army without profanity couldn't fight its way out of a piss-soaked paper bag. "

If you are the delicate sort, if plain talk offends you, you may be reading the wrong book. Perhaps I can write a children's version for you later. But I am a 23-year Navy veteran. When I was earning my stripes - some of them twice, but that's a different story - it was the guy who didn't drink, cuss or smoke that people didn't get too close to. They were the odd ones. I am an unapologetic product of that world. I also think people can be real pussies about words.

After the first iteration of this book, I was directly challenged on this point. Why do you actually have such expletives in the book? There are a few points here.

The same type of thinking that goes into demands for political correctness goes to our getting lathered up over certain words. I will stipulate that dropping an F-bomb in conversation can be an act of intellectual laziness.

But an F-bomb is also an expletive, called such for a reason. When taking on a system as sclerotic and corrupt as our government, one may use the term "gosh darn it" to express frustration. The problem here is **all** readers or listeners will immediately and instinctively think *he really meant god damn it.* The distractions are that the speaker is not emoting genuinely and the listener is making a needless thesaurus conversion. Result: weakened message.

I want politicians and apathetic voters to feel the weight of my words.

Still, it might be time we overcame our superstitions about magic words. Like all other vices, familiarity reduces fascination and thereby reduces proliferation. With less fascination about magic words, we'll actually see fewer of them, over time, not more.

My approach here will be the same as Patton's. If I try to be too sweet and pure, I will betray one of the bedrock principles this book promotes which is to **be yourself**, warts and all. But I would also write a very forgettable book. Who's to say I haven't anyway? But I'm not going to help you forget it. I'm gonna get in your head, dude.

1 GROWING A PAIR

"You ain't gotta stand tall in here. But you've got to stand up."
- Butcher, **An Innocent Man***, 1989*

"Do your damnedest in an ostentatious manner all the time."
- George S. Patton

Communicate much?

My biggest complaint against Republicans is they don't have a message. But truth be told, there is no way to know if they do or not. It is possible we have elected too many stupid people into positions of authority who couldn't communicate the instructions to a paint-by-number kit. What I suspect is more likely is they simply don't have the cojones to commit to a message and state it clearly for fear someone might call them on it.

But guys, and Carly, if you are not a mental midget like Boehner; you *want* to be called on your positions. The more you talk (and often piss people off) the more press you get. That means more opportunities to pound away at your message. Embrace the challenge! Argue your point! Lean in! Touch noses! Answer the question asked in such a way as to advance your argument; don't equivocate!

Liberals have a message that is almost without exception emotionalist, populist and easily dispelled. Picture Bill Clinton's wife bouncing in her chair like a fat, bratty kid yelling, "What difference does it make?" And yet they are successful.

Do you know why? It is because they take the fight to the camera, the microphone, the crowd, and the press. They know the louder they yell, the more baseless and emotionalist they are, the more mileage they'll get. And do you know why *that* is? It is because they know up until the printing of this book, there was no one on the other side willing to slap them down; more importantly to slap them down with sound thinking, not just a populist rant pulling in the opposite direction.

Let's take Billary's idiotic rant in front of the Congressional committee investigating Benghazi. A handler wrote it for her. She was instructed to use it when she ran out of bullshit to heap on the committee. Clearly, they were trying to have a Joe Welch/Joe McCarthy moment…"Have you no sense of decency, sir? At long last, have you left no sense of decency?" Leave aside the fact McCarthy ended up falling far short of the number of Soviet-friendly people we actually **did have** in the State department and throughout the government at that time. [1,2] Further, set aside the contrived, nakedly embarrassing and out of context quality of Rodham's moment. Instead, ask yourself why every Republican (and not a few Democrats) didn't go to the nearest microphone, camera or DC tour group and excoriate that foolish woman. Why did they not point out that such a remark is not only an insult to those she had killed in Benghazi, but a reiteration of her incompetence as Secretary of State, the Administration's fecklessness in foreign affairs, and a blatant demonstration of her inability to communicate *anything* honestly? Why did they not point out that her performance before the committee was a waste of their time and the taxpayers' money?

There are two answers. One is that these hearings are all theater anyway. The questions, and almost always the answers, are usually agreed to ahead of time. The more powerful the person in the hot seat, the more choreographed the show. This does not apply to our purposes here, but will make for a good book later. Keep an eye out for that.

The other reason is that before issuing a statement on the whole ugly mess, legislators were cautioned by their own handlers that they don't want to be seen picking on the cow because after all, she's just a girl. There are always a blizzard of reasons Republicans give for going easy on some creep sitting before them in a committee hearing. But they all spell the same thing. W-U-S-S-Y!

Wake up, people! The Democrats don't hush up when they have something like this handed to them. They swing for the fences! They have veins popping out of the faces. They go all red-faced and passionate. The female Clinton handed the Republicans the perfect tool with which to legitimately thrash her in the press and more importantly in debates and stump speeches. They still can. But will they?

It remains to be seen. I can only hope this book and perhaps the works of others in the *very near* future provide the GOP with the requisite sack to "stand up."

How to Stand Up

Okay, so you are a Republican aspiring to

high office. You've read the passage above and say to yourself, "My god! This Jordan fellow is a genius! How can I set myself apart from the herd and make myself a household word?"

The exclamation is understandable. The answer to your question lies in your demeanor.

Throughout this book I will bang away at the lean-in-and-touch-noses approach to winning. But don't mistake that for the kind of angry blather Elisha Cummings embarrasses himself with when he doesn't actually have a point to make, or with general crankiness. If they don't like you, they won't vote for you. The idea is to be right and be likable. You achieve this through humor and a genuine interest in your audience and by **being yourself**.

Don't act like someone you are not. Don't pretend to be angry. If you could pull that off successfully, you'd be in Hollywood pulling down twelve million a picture. Be angry in the way you are naturally angry. Be challenging in the way you are naturally challenging. If you are coarse and gregarious, don't hide it. Use it to deliver your message in a believable way. Think of Tip O'Neal. If you are bookish and perhaps a bit effete, channel Pat Moynihan. Are you naturally soft-spoken? Look no further than Harry Reid for an example of success.

It is not an accident that all the above are Democrats. While usually disagreeing with the first two examples, I have always admired both of them. Tip was nobody's fool. He was every bit the hard, gruff guy you would see at the Speaker's chair. Moynihan always had the courage of his convictions. The one exception may be his waffling on Clinton/Lewinski. In the case of Reid, he's one of the smarmiest creeps to disgrace the Senate chamber. But he could say a lot and did some serious damage just by whimpering in the well. You should, by no means, emulate his lack of scruples. Still he is proof you don't need plastic hair and a Pepsodent smile to get elected – and reelected. You need you, you need a message and you need guts.

I use Democrat examples because they are better at packaging. We have the message on our side. We must package it so people will *want* to listen. And you do that by not only getting the average voter to walk into his house and say, "Damn! Did you hear what (insert GOP candidate here) said? I couldn't believe my ears!" Be right when you say it and be prepared to back it up.

In this, Christie, Fiorina and Walker are all light-years ahead of the pack. Fiorina doesn't back away from questions and she stays on message. More importantly, her message is a good one. She knows her facts. She embraces opportunities to engage.

Christie comes across as a WYSIWYG kind of guy. "Hey, how ya doin'. I'm from Jersey. Nice place. Got any pasta? You're a good guy. Don't piss me off or I'll beat the shit outta ya. " It isn't a folksy show. It's him. It has served him very well in the past. He also comes across as a big-hearted guy. That is why the Republicans shot themselves in the foot for freaking out about his treatment of Obama after Sandy hit the coast. They were two executives, facing a crisis, BOTH putting their best foot forward and putting petty shit aside for that moment. When the Billy Bobs on Facebook pitched a fit, the field should have come vehemently to Christie's defense. It would have demonstrated real class by everyone. Instead, too many hurt the Republican brand.

Scott Walker's persona is friendly but no nonsense. He can be funny and is very approachable. But being himself and taking on what people thought were popular targets, he demonstrated the greedy Union Leader has no clothes. Walker got reelected several times that way.

I am not endorsing these candidates. But as long as two of them don't step on their dicks and one doesn't get her boobs caught in a ringer, I think they will run some really great campaigns.

2 MESSAGE

"Of all the talents bestowed upon men, none is so precious as the gift of oratory. He who enjoys it wields a power more durable than that of a great king. He is an independent force in the world. "
- Winston Churchill

"We're going to get him by the balls and we're going to kick him in the ass..."
- George Patton (unedited) on winning.

What has happened to the American message? By that, I don't just mean what we say, but how we say it.

What we *do* say these days is problematic to begin with. I wouldn't give a plugged nickel for most of the texts I receive. There is so little intended. And even then it is poorly stated, usually misspelled and incorrectly punctuated, if punctuated at all. I feel I can say this because I make an effort to communicate a meaningful message, even when creating a friendly text.

This is doubly true when I exchange texts

with the nice lady who charges my credit card by the message. She loves me. She's working her way through medical school. Oh, smirk if you want to.

I hear people say our laptops and cell phones have destroyed our ability to communicate. And those things have done some serious damage. But the problem goes back much further. To see the genesis of the problem, you need to look at the two previous centuries side by side.

Nearly everyone has seen the documentary series *The Civil War* by Ken Burns. This was a masterful project based in part on *The Civil War – A Narrative* by Selby Foote, a historical epic. Throughout the series you hear quoted several letters written by soldiers, from Corporal to General, including the shattering love letter written by Sullivan Ballou to his wife, Sarah, the week before he died. To this very minute I can barely think of that letter without nearing tears. And I'm a cynical bastard.

It can be said about all these correspondents, that they made a clear effort to communicate. At the end of their letters, you knew their hearts and you knew their minds. I flatter myself to think I might convey a message half as well as they did.

Foote, himself, exemplifies this rich and

sincere communication. The epitome of a southern gentleman, he speaks in a quiet, unassuming tone. But his words carry luster. You could sit in a chair, sip sweet tea and listen to him for hours. There are others who provide this colorful clarity of expression; Hitchens, Will and Buckley leap to my mind since I have so much enjoyed their work over the years.

Sadly, such people are quite rare in our time. I believe this has been caused by distraction. Most of that is a product of our media. I don't mean that as criticism of the media as an industry - trust me, I'll do lots of that later – so much as a statement about passive listening and an overabundance of content.

If you read anything from the early to mid twentieth century, you start to see a slow slouching toward mediocrity, especially in personal letters, even schoolwork. The trend follows almost perfectly with the beginning of the industrial era, then the radio age and spirals downward as technology brings film, television and finally personal electronics. Now, just posting a hand-written letter is a lost social skill. The only people who send me actual letters are all older than me. For the record, I am somewhere between the ages of 29 and Stonehenge.

Modern politicians are not simply the product of this. Many are well educated and perfectly capable of concise, insightful communication. But they actively resist the use of these skills. They are counting on the fact that *you are* distracted. They complain about the thirty-second sound bite, but wouldn't trade it for the world. They use them to churn out polled buzzwords and ad hominem attacks on their opponents. *And by golly, if it wasn't for a lack of time they'd say more, but...*

So like the people I describe in the preface to this book, these politicians bend over backwards to not get into real discussions and possibly make a misstep. They try to get elected because they are the most popular and said the least number of constructive things during a campaign.

The candidate who will win this election **can be** the one who says what needs to be said, but as I mentioned at the beginning of this chapter, says it right.

Become the Standout! In This Environment, it's Laughably Easy!

Ty: ...Relax. Find your center. Picture the shot, Danny. Picture it! Turn off all the sound and just

*let it happen. Be the ball.... Be the ball, Danny....
You're not being the ball, Danny.*

*Danny: Well, it's difficult with you talking like
that.*

That movie was a gut buster when it came
out in 1980. Now, it's kind of embarrassing to
watch. But it serves us quite well here.

Before I have even put pen to paper – a nice
phase, but I'm using a laptop – the Republican
field has pretty much made itself known.
(Except for Piyush Jindal; his announcement is
expected in a day or two.3) They have all
followed the predictable pattern of big
announcement, hit the stump telling every state
that it is the most important one, and piss on
fellow Republicans. There are three notable
exceptions to the predictability. Carly Fiorina's
in-your-face trouncing of the woman who was
First Lady when Al Gore was Vice President, is
one. The fact that Chris Christie has released two
policy papers on foreign policy and the economy
before officially announcing his candidacy is
refreshing.4 Then there was Trump's
announcement, which looked like a splashy
opening of another casino. For Trump that is
perfectly predictable, for a Presidential

campaign, not so much.

But they are standing out and moving the polls right now. Why? Because to a varying degree, they are participating in or being featured by, that which usually distracts.

Be the distraction, Carly. Be the distraction!

Do you, the candidate, want a conservative victory in '16? How about '20 and '24? I am talking about Reagan traction here. Do you want your message to resonate? Do you want people to slap their forehead and wonder where you've been all of their voting years? *Be the distraction.*

Don't let a day go by without saying something that will rattle the press or give them the vapors. It will rarely get favorable coverage. That's not important. I'll get to handling the press in a bit. The point is you will be a major part of more news cycles than your opponents.

Another word might be disruption. With every leap forward in technology, there is a disruption in the economy. The thickheaded decry it every time.

Before I tell the candidates how to be the distraction or be the disruption, let me wax anecdotal to sharpen the point.

During the 2012 election, when Republicans, once again snatched defeat from the jaws of victory, Mitt Romney put in an appearance at a Wawa store. If you live on the East Coast you know what I am talking about.

I made a passing reference about Wawa stores in my blog last year.5

After his visit, Romney made a fuss about the efficiency and convenience of buying lunch there. You just use the touch screen device at the deli counter, pour yourself a cup of amazing coffee6 and, bingo, you have a big, fresh hoagie waiting for you.

The press went batshit over it. Their take away was that Romney was out of touch to be so enamored with such technology. For one thing, touch screens are commonplace. For another, such screens put people out of work. And, as usual when talking about a conservative, they got it all wrong and that was probably intentional. But, so what? Several important things happened as a result of Romney's praise of a simple business model. He got two days of press talking about "these Wawass" as he called them, and the viewer knew what he was talking about despite what the press was trying to make of it.

While these touch screens are commonplace, they are not common in convenience stores or restaurants. Also, they do not put people out of work. Go to a Wawa. Then go to the nearest 7-11.

Look at the cleanliness, efficiency, quality of employee, and **number** *of employees. Wawa took the convenience store business model and improved it in every aspect. (There are still lots of 7-11s where you can't use a restroom.) The fresh deli and efficient ordering allows Wawa to hire twice the workers you would find in other convenience stores. They don't do it out of the kindness of their hearts, that isn't worth a bucket of warm spit. It is because they need employees to keep pace with all the customers they bring in and keep – forever.*

"These Wawass" were an industry disruption. It led to Turkey Hill improving their stores, and the arrival of the Kangaroo Stores that dot the gulf coast. And people, for two days, got to see Romney **correctly** *praising that model. And when talking about an industry disruption, he became a political disruption himself. And he was part of the distraction in the political news; not the drone or the white noise nobody gives a shit about anymore.*

Here's the best part. He didn't do it on purpose. He was just **being himself.** *Rule number ONE.*

The secret to capitalizing on rule number one and being the distraction is to think twice and then say what you are thinking. Say it clearly. Look and sound like you are in the moment. Better yet, be in the moment. This is most true when dealing with subjects conservatives *should* be talking about. And they are the subjects that will get you the most mileage.

I will dedicate a little space to several of these subjects. It will be, by no means, a complete list. But they will make a splash if used properly. By properly, I mean aggressively.

The Truth is Your Friend!

It has long been the "trick" of what was considered a "good" politician to say as little as possible while blathering on for seconds, minutes or hours. BJ Bill is the king. He can, and has droned for two and a half hours, never uttering a single meaningful phrase.

To the politicians and their handlers: *Everybody knows this now.* We are bone weary of it. We are left trying to decipher what the hell you just said to see if you are worth a damn. The empty rhetoric is not impressive. It stands between you, your message and your audience. Tear away that filter!

Would you like to cement your Congressional seat or the presidency right now?

Would you like to have loooong coat tails? Would you like to see yourself and other conservatives winning in 2016, 2020, 2024? Then pay attention!

To win battles, and he won more than anyone, Patton said you have to get the enemy by the balls and kick him in the ass. Among the cocktail party/diplomat generals coming of age in Patton's time, his approach was seen as uncivilized. That's why Patton swept more than halfway across France while Monty was in Calais gathering mountains of supplies preparing to pounce - I swear you can't make this stuff up – like a "ferocious rabbit".

Unless you define victory as, "we'll all just whisper sweetly and I hope I win", you understand that **certain** victory belongs to the audacious. You have to get your opponents *and* the voter by the balls, but in different ways and for different reasons. (Important reminder here: the key opponent is anyone with a D after her or his name. We're not about fratricide. I'll deal with that later.)

I can tell you with diamond-tip certainty that the American voter is ready and waiting for the politician who will slap them across the face with brutal honesty. When you get the voters by the balls, it isn't to defeat them. You want to let them know, in no uncertain terms that you are the new breed of kick-ass, in-your-face politician. To do that you will need two things.

A stump speech loaded with hard, honest, conservative truth and an equally honest elevator speech laced with language coarse *or evocative* enough to get your message in the news every fucking day.

Does that mean *you* have to say the F-word? Of course not. The truth is usually shattering enough to make you the distraction from the white noise.

Why do you think Trump entered the race at number two in the polls and a candidate like Bobby Jindal, an excellent candidate, is at the bottom? It is because Trump spews true and/or audacious statements like a fire hose. He called Perry on his ham-handed plane hangar announcement speech. No one else even thought to do it. And he was right. He happily delineates between Latino citizens and immigrants versus illegals. It put him front and center in the race coverage. The leftwing Latinos, who still stupidly think progressivism is good for their community, are in an uproar. Trump is reveling in that. He speaks the truth and people love it!

Even Fox News snickered behind their hands when Trump said he would bring the jobs home from places like China. How, asks Dana Perino (the naïve Polly Purebred of The Five) can he bring back jobs from China? For someone who surrounds herself with conservatives, that is a monumentally stupid question.

BUT, addressing that very question gives *ANY* conservative candidate the opportunity to put into their stump speech an outline to explain exactly how *they* will do it.

Better still for the brave; most candidates don't have the guts to do so. They think declaring a tax holiday on repatriated money will be seen as a program for the rich. That must mean it is bad for the poor, right? Wrong. Let's say we tell people with money overseas that they can bring it home and not get pounded with taxes. Tell them that we are lowering the corporate tax rate. Up to two and a half trillion dollars comes washing in. Do you think this cash will be hidden in mattresses? Of course not! It will be spent and invested. And that means jobs! Lots of them!

But that's a compound thought process. Your more gutless opponents are also the mentally slower. That leaves the ones who are smarter than Trump and gutsier than the rest to make a huge splash. If you think you need to spell these things out to people in your presentations, bring a dry-erase board and an easel! You can't help but be more engaged and engaging when you start to illustrate your points, however crudely, in this way. The press will pan it. Your target audience will eat it up!

By now the voter and the candidate who sees himself[7] in these pages can imagine an event where he is **being himself**. He is interacting with the crowd. If he's using that whiteboard, he's got marker stains on his hands and maybe his tie. He is laughing almost as hard at his own jokes as the audience because he is *engaged and in the moment.* His shtick isn't canned crap. He is free. He is puking truth all over the stage.

And here's the best part. Tomorrow, when the press blows an aneurism because you were so *out there* in front of voters, and they try to diminish your points one by one, *you will not apologize or minimize one bit.* You will be using the critiques as they come to further advance your argument, point by point. You will announce that you had so much fun last night that you will double down on the process next time.

Of all the candidates in the race, Bobby Jindal has the advantage here. Of all the announcement speeches, his was head and shoulders above the rest in terms of his **being himself**, being in the moment and lovin' on the crowd. He sounded great. He should crank it up two or three notches. Christie has a bit of it too, with the happy tough-guy routine. It's very likable.

Disadvantage goes to Kasich and Santorum. They are nice guys but don't spark the imagination. Of course, they haven't read this book yet. Also Huckabee struggles here. He couldn't pull off "sincere" for love or money. That's why he has to play the god card again and again.

But It's Not All Fun and Games, Is It?

While you are out there relatin' and yuckin' it up and getting sweat rings down to your waistband, you must keep your primary objective in mind. To win! And in order to win, you must teach. You must reawaken a sense of citizenship in your audience. You don't have to teach them to be Republicans (the party); you have to teach them to be republicans (members of American society). You teach the latter, you get the former.

As a serious contender, there are only two times a year when you should be teaching; when the circus is in town and when it ain't. (For those who think Huck is a conservative, that means the winning candidate is always teaching.) The subjects to be taught, as I said, will be covered later. But if you are an honest candidate or an informed voter, you already know what those chapters are about. If you can't guess correctly what they'll be about by now, but get to the end of the book, I can only say welcome to the real world and I hope you enjoy the ride.

There was a time when large doses of teaching were not as important as being erudite and/or interesting. Those days are gone, my friends. We live in a world where people think they are voting for monarchs or gods. There are far too many voters who believe that Obama really knows how many tenths of a degree the earth's temperature will drop by wrecking the energy industry and the economy. They are so impressed with this "knowledge" they are actually grateful that he is trying to do it. (By that I mean he is really trying to wreck the economy. He knows that you can't really predict the temperature change with any degree of accuracy, up or down.) The voters who are so enamored with their candidate, especially the Presidential candidates, have a warped view of what the office is. They believe the term "the most powerful man on the planet" means their guy is imbued with almost mystic powers over everything. They don't understand that it is a relative term reflecting his advantage as chief executive of a rich republic who can field the most advanced military. It doesn't mean he is actually **all-powerful**.

We'll pause a moment to let the suddenly disenchanted, stupid people catch their breath.

Even people you wouldn't think of as dull-witted have used the words "running the country" when referring to Presidents and "our leaders" when referring to legislators. It's no wonder the people inside the beltway think so highly of themselves. 8

Senators have people bowing and scraping before them in committee hearings. Legislators will say things to a witness that would earn them a punch in the face in any other setting, and this almost always being politically motivated. When they have real scumbags like Lois Learner or Mrs. Rodham-Clinton in front of them – *mostly* puffballs. And not only do Presidents actually think they were elected to "run the country" and Congressmen think of themselves as "leaders", the Four Morons of the American apocalypse9 actively encourage the distortion by ceding their constitutional authority and relevance to the oval office.

While the latter are the worst offenders ever,

this has been going on for a long time. So the first order of business is to teach what used to be grammar school civics to voting adults.

Be sure to discuss truth in advertising with your audience as often as possible. Whenever an opponent promises to pass school prayer or an abortion in every pot, pounce! Use the opportunity to let the voter know that they are the arbiters of what is to go on in Washington DC and in their own lives. Citizens are perfectly capable of running their own lives and businesses and therefore the country just fine without the kind of "help" our DC gods have on offer.

So now we have an idea of how to grab the voter by the balls. Lets drill down a bit *before* we go after our opponents both Republican and Democrat.

3 CONSERVATIVE

"Oh, there's nothing better for American conservatism than periodic examples of untrammeled liberalism. "
- George Will, therightscoop.com, 10 Jan 14
"The difference between a liberal and a conservative is that the liberal thinks we should be equal at the finish line while conservatives think we should be equal at the starting line. "
- Barry Goldwater, Jr., Washingtontimes.com 17 Nov 14

The world is turned upside down. Never have two opposing political camps been more inaccurately mislabeled. When you get a chance, take a gander at Merriam Webster.com. Number 5 in the expanded definition of a liberal is ": broad-minded; especially: not bound by authoritarianism, orthodoxy, or traditional forms. [Emphasis theirs]

That may be so in the long-dead, Jeffersonian sense. But in the case of the modern American liberal10(or progressive as they love being known) there is no animal more pig-headed. No one is more enamored with the idea of big government, authoritarianism and orthodoxy than the modern American liberal. And a big, fat government we do have. The Emperor FDR himself could never have imagined the reach of government into our lives that we have today. This, even as convinced as he was that he was the smartest, most evolved creature on wheels.

Despite the fact that big-government liberalism has failed miserably at every turn, libs remain dogmatically devoted to its survival. There is no idea, other than "liberal" doctrine that is acceptable. And the only way to keep big government alive is through ever-growing authoritarianism.

Now, at the same website, look at the definition of conservative. Number 3a is almost comical: "tending or disposed to maintain existing views, conditions, or institutions. Number 3c describes me brilliantly; "taste, elegance, style..."

The fact is, those now labeled as "conservatives" have blazed the trail since the 1950's toward equal rights, better education, responsible government and making room for the individual to thrive. Libs now like to cry about the 80s and say it was the decade of greed. But it was the very concepts put into play in the 80s that let libs graduate from dirty jeans to New York condos. By contrast, liberals in that same timeframe have destroyed education, turned equal rights into a populist ghetto, put half the population on food stamps and demanded the individual surrender to the Borg...er, uh... the collective.

Before I get into a definition of what the modern, successful, politically viable conservative is today, let me humbly suggest what he is not.

Not!

He is not a doctrinaire. Despite the label "conservative", he is not afraid to swim against the current. Just because powerful people in his own camp cling to an idea, that doesn't bind him. He is a freethinking, open-minded individual.

He is not male (the grammatical convenience often used here not withstanding). Look at Carly Fiorina, Nikki Haley – who should be running for the oval office, look at Megan Kelly. Look at her a lot. It's fun.

Nor is she white. I give you Chrystal Wright, aka Conservative Black Chick, Condoleezza Rice, the most powerful woman in American History,

Stacy Dash (I want to be her stalker). At the risk of sounding cliché, some of the best-informed conservatives I know are female and black. One of my favorite people in the world, Jessica Burns (gutsy entrepreneur-type), is always the smartest person in the room, if not a bit silly at times. Very conservative. And just to put a fine point on it, she is pro gay marriage.

He is not straight. We not only have Log Cabin Republicans, there are strong individual gay voices in the conservative camp. Christopher R. Barron and Jimmy LaSalvia are founders of GOProud.

He is not Christian. Although there is a part of the Conservative movement that believes their Christianity is interwoven with their conservatism, most do not conflate religious beliefs with political issues and aspirations. Conservatives come from every religious background. And get this: A lot of conservatives are Atheists "...dogs sleeping with cats! Mass hysteria!"

A conservative is NOT a single-issue voter. Scratch the surface of a "conservative" who can only vote for a candidate who sees life through one issue (gay marriage, abortion, global warming, school prayer), and you'll find a person with a narrow mind and an overblown sense of entitlement and self. In other words, a liberal who is too dumb to know he is actually a liberal. There are exceptions to this rule. When the "single issue" cuts a swath through the very fabric on which this nation was built, like Obamacare, tyrannical behavior of the Chief Executive, or war, then you may have single issues that will withstand scrutiny.

We are not jealous of what another has. That's petty and leads to diminishing self-respect. We celebrate the success of others and try to emulate the practices of successful people in order to be more successful ourselves. By all means, if the richest guy in town has things or does things that you'd like to have or do, let his life serve as motivation and remind you that you will be there one day as well...if you are as willing to work as hard or harder than he has. 11

A conservative is not racist. You will see me, more than once, in this august tome, refer to Billy Bob. He's the mouth-breathing Walmartian who thinks conservatism is a about hating minorities, lovin' Jesus, drinking Jack Daniels, listening to country music, wishing the South had won the war, owning a Nazi flag and dating your sister. 12 This is one of the two stereotypes of conservatives invented by the media and kept alive by rich, morbid obese, ignorant, Hollywood "documentarians". 13 The other image is that of the rich guy who loves that people suffer while he sits and counts his money over and over again.

I'm going to spend a bit of time with Billy Bob because it is important to dispel phony notions and because it's fun.

There really are people who think they are conservative because they hate minorities (like Robert Byrd did – I know, the irony is so thick you can smell it). These are not conservatives in any form that furthers any real argument or leaves the world or a community any better off. They're not Eisenhower conservatives. His administration authored the Civil Rights Act. Johnson finally got it passed after dragging a handful of Dems to the table kicking and screaming.

They are not Reagan types. The Billy Bobs of this world never had the guts to get a decent job, much less stake their claim in this world.

They're not W conservatives. W's hallmark legislation was No Child Left Behind. Billy Bobs can't read as well as most children and don't care to.

And the whole Nazi, skinhead thing; Christ! Hitler was first and foremost a socialist! But we have Hollywood, and Billy Bob himself, saying that Billy Bob is conservative.

Give me a break. Here's a thought: The GOP is called the big tent. We welcome everybody. Okay, fine. Can we consider chasing Billy Bob to the other side? He can't read a ballot anyway. Or at least have him take a bath?

What a Conservative IS...

The following is somewhat subjective. It's based on years of reading the works of conservatives and liberals, judging the validity of their commentary and monitoring results. I have condensed all this into a basic, workable concept of conservatism.

A good conservative is informed. We gather information from multiple sources. We know our own camp and know our opponent. There is no way to check one's own beliefs from inside the echo chamber. If you read the Drudge Report and consider yourself aware of your world[14], you are a lame conservative.

Along that same line, a good conservative doesn't accept something just because a politician or celebrity says it is so.

A good conservative is responsible. If you have a family, you provide for them (that includes accidental family, even if you don't marry the mother). You leave a place as good or better than you found it. You provide for your own retirement. You involve yourself in the community and schools.

With responsibility comes self-reliance. We are more interested in what we can accomplish, in pursuit of our daily bread, than we are having bread handed to us.

A conservative demands (or should demand) facts. These are the things we need to decide what we will support or reject. For example, there are 47 federal job training programs being paid for by productive citizens. Many have not graduated a single applicant. Most have not resulted in a single job. There are no matrices to measure the progress of these programs. Just last week the White House proposed yet another job training program. No one inside the beltway has a clue what job skills are in demand right now. This Byzantine circus is among many that have to be ended. There are no facts to justify their existence. What's more, we have to do a better job of monitoring these and all bureaucratic boondoggles. They need to be set right, drastically cut back or shut down.

A conservative wants legislators and executives that govern according to the law. What is made legal for one must be legal for all. What is denied one (one state, one race, one school, one person) must be denied all.

A good conservative loves and understands the new blood immigration brings to the market. LEGAL immigration. "What is legal for one..." right? People who wish to come to this country are required by law to go through a process. We don't need new laws. We just have to enforce existing law. Make the legal process as safe and effective as possible. And make life for those here illegally as uncomfortable as legally possible. The problem then solves itself.

A good conservative is a conservationist. Not the tofu and granola kind - the real kind. You take care of your world. You don't throw your crap on the ground like they do at Earth Day rallies. You hunt and fish, but not indiscriminately. And you don't need a beltway lawyer to define "indiscriminately" for you. The world is an asset. You didn't have to purchase it, but you occupy a part of it. Referring back to the paragraph on responsibility, you leave your world a better place than how you found it. It is the least mark you can leave as a human being as well.

A conservative doesn't want his representatives to "bring home the bacon". He wants them to leave more of the citizen's own, earned bacon at home to begin with.

A conservative absolutely understands the need for a social safety net for those on hard times. A safety net, not a pillow upon which one lounges for life. And that safety net should be sustenance and shelter. No one should be able to draw cash at an ATM with a food stamp card. They should only work at supermarkets for the purchase of critical foodstuffs. They shouldn't finance Pringles or high-end running shoes. Wider welfare programs should work the same way.

We also believe in human dignity. That isn't found in an unearned life, but in the value of what one does for oneself.

4 ISSUES

Politicians trim and tack in their quest for power, but they do so in order to get the wind of votes in their sails.
-Ian Gilmour

Dump the Phony Issues

Fortunately, for the true conservative candidate, legitimate issues are few.   But you wouldn't know it looking at a modern campaign. Remember when I said that too many people in this country LOVE to be lied to? I also said the many think they are electing an emperor to repair their lives for them.   They're candidate, like God, is on their side. I hate to burst your obscene bubbles troops, but neither of them is. Whatever your concept of a god, he would be a bit busy controlling a universe. It is at once petty and arrogant in the extreme to think he is out there sweating whether Al Pacino Middle School in the Bronx has school prayer or teaches evolution. The candidate is equally busy on the temporal plane. The difference is that the politician will lie and pretend he is interested. Gods tend to remain rather mute.

Now keep in mind that I am talking about candidates for **federal office**. They know such issues and others like local police matters, local tax issues, etc. are not things they should get involved in. The guy running for mayor or county supervisor better damned sure get involved in them. They should be the busiest officials in your life. DC legislators and the President ought to be the least known or heard from.

Federal legislators and the President are not judges. They don't know anything about your town. They have no idea of local tradition, much less your local laws. There is a GOOD reason why the voter should embrace this reality. It is the same reason those geniuses back in 1787 limited the scope of our government. The people in South Bend, Indiana are competent enough to decide, if the issue were to be raised, whether to fly the American flag in front of their schools. If Spotsylvania, Virginia decided to enact an ordinance saying that no illegal aliens can work in their county, that's their business. If your town says that they are going to ban multiple partner marriage, and you happen to favor that ordinance, do you want some schmuck from DC telling you it must be otherwise? Are you all such idiots that you cannot deal with these things without turning to the grand, imperial, magical gods on Mount Bullshit to wipe the drool from your chins?

Of course not!

Besides, we are often surprised by the results of such pleadings, aren't we? Justice Roberts, just recently, stepped into the well (metaphorically speaking) and changed the Obama administration's arguments for them. The subject was Obamacare. The pro-socialized medicine crowd had the loosing argument. Roberts, as he did when the administration's arguments contradicted themselves the last time, changed the meaning of our language and in a tortured piece of case law, made a ruling based on his new fantasy argument. 15

But until that very moment, anti-Obamacare voters were saying, *finally, we are saved from Obamacare because the court couldn't possibly let this one go by.* And yet they did. And so it is with social issues. You don't want them to bubble to the surface inside the beltway. They'll pretzel it beyond recognition and then often disappoint you. Keep local and personal issues local and personal. Don't feed the federal pig with excuses to get into your lives.

Beyond disappointment is the fact that by dabbling in such issues, including the popular ones, they are exercising a form of tyranny the constitution intended they not. The federal government has few responsibilities; defense, foreign relations and interstate trade. They cock that up along with everything else they touch because they, with the help of the courts, have gotten their greasy meat hooks into almost every aspect of our lives. By ignoring their constitutional mandate, they have created an incompetent, overloaded leviathan. It doesn't work and costs too much because no organization, no party, no person can involve itself in so much and succeed. So the candidate who will put the Republicans, and more importantly conservatives, on a long-term winning streak is the guy who says that he is out of the social issues business.

Who has the guts to say that if a bill is sent to the White House dealing with bullying,16 *it will be vetoed and the authors will be called out and ridiculed? Get the cameras and microphones ready! Tune up your crybaby voice, Chris Matthews! Here's the winning candidates take: HEY, PARENTS! RAISE BETTER KIDS! I AM NOT THE BABYSITTER-IN-CHIEF!* A legislative hopeful can make the same pledge to excoriate anyone who introduces bills that are outside the scope of federal authority which assume helplessness on the part of American adults to raise *their* kids or live *their* lives.

Gay Marriage, as an Example

This is the phony issue of phony issues. It also demonstrates how shallow too many of us are in our dealings with the wider world.

Militant gays seem to get an almost erotic thrill from destroying the lives of people who don't see life **exactly** as they do. A baker might say, "You know, I won't be able to work your wedding because it is against my religious beliefs. " The normal person may take exception to being turned down by a vendor, but there are countless others out there. So finding one is a simple process.

But what did the perpetually offended just such a situation? They did whatever they could to ruin the livelihood and thereby the lives of the religiously conscientious baker. What lowlifes! What ass hats! And it isn't lost on me that the whole thing might have been a setup in the first place so some activists could gain some cred with fellow crazies within the gay community. And how could they even hope to be successful at that? It is because this country has made interpersonal relationships the purview of politics and the state. If we weren't busy codifying what a relationship is there would be no one to cry to if a person says I don't want to participate in an activity that I strongly disagree with.

Which leads to my next point. Issues like gay marriage are where politicians go when they find that a) they don't have any real ideas to discuss, b) want to pander to one segment of the population at the expense of another. To these politicians, specifically conservatives,17 may I humbly suggest you mind your own goddamn business? What the hell do you care if Maggie and Mary want to get married? The true answer is: you don't. In a different context, you'd be kissing Maggie and Mary's butts for votes like you would anyone else's. So stick to the issues we'll be dealing with in future chapters of this weighty tome and don't muddy the waters with crap about who can make a commitment to whom.

To both sides of this argument: Marriage is a sacrament. It is a throwback to a time when the church was the government. Marriage was a tool for the church to try to cement its control over succeeding generations of their congregation. It also showed them where their new congregants would be coming from. In other words it was about maintaining power and money. And that is the reason it remained a part of the secular governments that replaced the church.

Here it comes...*so you're saying we should ignore 1000 years of tradition?*

I do hear that often. Tradition is a lousy reason to make law. It is certainly NO reason for the government to concern itself with people's personal affairs. Honor killings are a tradition. Arranged marriages are a tradition. Clitorectomies are a tradition. Does tradition make them any less stupid or uncivilized?

Traditions will inevitably give way to advancement. That is a simple fact. Some traditions are kept simply for the enjoyment of the practitioners. But they are not cast in stone. C'mon guys. Did you **not** see *Fiddler on the Roof?*

There are probably dozens of such ideas that can viewed through the same prism: flag burning, book burning, Koran burning, TV nudity, online gambling... The "Leader of the Free World" and the Congress that writes the laws he must follow, have far more important issues to deal with. Especially when you realize how many of these phony issues we need to flush out of the existing system. So grow up America and own your shit! We're not going to deal with it for you anymore.

Take this attitude and win!

Voters: If you see this kind of a person in a candidate, vote for that person! You'll be happier four years from now that you did.

But there is more to consider. You may see much of what is to follow in some of our candidates (if they ever emerge) so voting for them will be easy.

5 OTHER PEOPLE'S MONEY

"One of the great debates of our time is about how much of your money should be spent by the State and how much you should keep to spend on your family. Let us never forget this fundamental truth: the State has no source of money other than money which people earn themselves. If the State wishes to spend more it can do so only by borrowing your savings or by taxing you more. It is no good thinking that someone else will pay— that "someone else" is you. There is no such thing as public money; there is only taxpayers' money. "
- Margaret Thatcher

"The problem with socialism is that you eventually run out of other people's money.
- Margaret Thatcher

Before we get to the nut of it...

The discussion about how the government siphons off your money is not all about taxes, you see. For example, interests rates have been held artificially low for years now. This has two, and only two reasons. One is to make easy money available to Wall Street and big banks. The other is to provide the government an easy means to service debt and acquire new debt. As I'll say elsewhere, your government competes directly against you for every dime of available credit. Not only that, if your finances looked 1/100th as bad as the government's, you wouldn't qualify for a loan. But the government does.

Further, by keeping interests rates artificially low, the Fed cheats you out of several percentage points of interest. The interest in your bank account doesn't even keep pace with inflation. If the interest rates were market driven and based on demand for cash or credit, you would be making more in interest. So the government gets to irresponsibly continue to borrow money at your direct expense now and your future expense when it comes time to pay the piper for all that government debt. Lucky you!

Let's Get Down To It!

We conservatives talk a great game when it comes to tax reform. But we rarely follow through. It's the same with profligate spending. Those we've voted in only trim around the edges on these things. In the meantime our economy has slowly withered. The success of small and medium sized businesses has occurred not because of what the Beltway whores have done, but despite it. Imagine where we'd all be right now if those businesses didn't have to contend with a bureaucracy that spends its time writing regulations that favor a chosen few of the "bigs. " Almost to the last one, these regulations have the intent of interfering with the companies that compete with the well connected.

Between a monstrous government and the crony class it supports (that's called corruption) we dance on the precipice of losing it all. More and more people are giving up, apathy is at an all-time high, productivity is floundering and growth has been a joke for years. We are very close to having more takers than makers in our economy. We are not only losing jobs to other countries, we are losing corporations as well.

This is the perfect time to change all that. The Progressives have never been so discredited. The vast majority of Americans are beginning to awaken to this. But to do it right, to actually turn the ship around will take an extra athletic effort from a candidate, soon-to-be elected official, with guts and grit.

But that candidate will first, have a lot of

work to do changing what citizens *think* they know about the nature of taxes and government spending.

We'll get to the spending later. But for now, the most important point you can hammer home is that government spending, as it exists today, can never give you as much as you can provide for yourself. If you are working middle class, you will never see a benefit commensurate with what you pay into this malfunctioning system.

If you look to the government for anything, thinking you benefit in the long run, you are a sucker (the exception being anyone who truly **cannot** do for themselves). And if a real conservative emerges and takes this country where it needs to go, suckers who try to hold onto the government tit by cheating will be left behind and will deserve every misfortune that will come with that decision.

That said, lets discuss where the governing class gets the money it wastes every year.

And before anyone gets their panties in a wad about the tax cuts and simplification we will discuss, I'll tip my hand now. We are going to scatter most of the IRS to the far corners of government and fire the rest. So now you don't even need to ask.

The Ugly Truth

Of this entire book, this is the section that will be most lied about, in order to discredit the message. Although I will write in later chapters that considerations must be carved out for those in true need, commentators will say that the plans I discuss will be designed to hurt the poor and favor the rich. Even though the numbers I use will be uniform for all income levels, the peanut gallery will still say that the plans will hurt the middle class. And they will say the same about you if you adopt any of it. But don't worry. Most people will know the progressive commentators are full of shit.

Truth #1

Corporations pay no taxes. They just don't. It may look like they do on paper, but they pay no taxes. Taxes are factored into the cost of doing business. They know where they want to be in a year; their financial picture, shares, sales, debt, etc. When they calculate all this, they also calculate future taxes and they note how they came out against past taxes. That all goes into what they charge the customer. If a dime of taxes comes out of intended profit or the shareholders' cut, that is considered bad management. So when the government says that JC Penny must pay a 30% rate before write-offs, who do you think pays that? The customers, of course. You. You pay JC Penny's taxes, the wholesaler's taxes, the manufacturers' taxes and so on.

And so it is with all for-profit companies. You, the reader, the voter, pays for it all. In fact a great deal of the debt you carry went to pay other peoples taxes. Then you pay your own taxes. And it's all perfectly legal. If you think about it, it cannot possibly work any other way. In a lock-step communist state, whatever business is allowed to eek out a living, will still pay no taxes. They will decide what they can make from a product. They will then calculate the tax burden and charge their customers extra to cover that bill.

Now, the shareholders and the board of directors and employees of the company do pay taxes on their personal income. But when a member of the board of JC Penny buys a lawn mower from Home Depot, he is also paying Home Depot's taxes for them. And since it is likely that he can buy a nice zero-turning radius riding mower, the mower will cost more. So he will not only pay more retail cost and sales tax, he'll carry a bigger share of Home Depot's corporate taxes. This compared to say, me and my 22-inch walk behind mower.

Perhaps I'll deal later with the added insult of paying a company's taxes while they are also getting federal subsidies. Yeah, you paid for that too.

So how do we avoid spending so much of our money for the direct benefit of companies, large and small? First you get rid of the goodies the government provides at our expense. All of them! ALL. OF. THEM. That too will be discussed in future chapters. Then you do what will make the liberals go out of their minds; and make the average "conservative" candidate pass urine. You slash the corporate tax.

There's more, of course. But let's stay here for a minute. Many of you just dropped the book on the floor and have to get your breathing and heart rate back to normal before we move on.

One deep cleansing breath, and...sigh. Okay! Let's dive in.

To understand how we will all benefit from this you must think dynamically. You must shed all the progressive dogma the media has been excreting on you since FDR. You must see this clearly in your mind as it unfolds.

Candidates, you must get hot with the whiteboard or PowerPoint when discussing this.

Handlers, shut the hell up for a few days! The American people are not stupid. Most people will get this; enough to get your man elected. And it WILL work!

Karl Rove, have a sandwich, eat your tie, I don't know...choke yourself. But shut up! You know better than anyone that this is a GREAT move and will set the economy on fire.

The First Reason to Say, "Why the hell not?"

Well-connected businesses such as GE, Aetna, and big Wall Street firms not only don't really pay taxes; they are not charged the same taxes as other companies. Why would they be? They actually get to **write the laws** that cover their industry.18 As a result, they can use this reduced overhead cost to beat out competitors.

So benefit number one of radically reduced corporate tax for everyone is that companies will be competing on an even playing field. Take whatever the federal corporate tax is at the moment and reduce it to ten percent. That will be the reduction in the markup companies will charge for their goods and services. The discount could be substantial, but as you will see, inconsequential in the larger scheme of things. No matter. It *will* work.

The Second Reason

And no, they won't keep charging you the old prices and hide the money in a mattress. They will want to compete as they always have. They will want a loyal customer base. They will chop their prices as far as the market will bear.

There will be companies who won't see that much difference in their tax rate anyway. Established companies, and medium and large companies, are very careful to maintain the expenses and infrastructure in such a way as to maximize write-offs. So in many cases while the corporate tax rate may be 30%, the effective tax rate is much lower. With compliance costs and government inefficiency on policing all this money, it will turn out that the government won't lose nearly as much as you might think in this scenario. If you are old enough to recall the repeal of the boat tax and luxury tax, it is not inconceivable that within a year or two the tax receipts will be higher than they are with the present tax rate. We are getting rid of all the write-offs and gimmicks.

Now We Take All The Power From the Progressives!

Kill the income and payroll tax withholding.

BJ Bill's old lady just threw up in her high fiber cereal. Karl Rove is pecking out talking points and telling anyone who will listen that this is too controversial.

I didn't say to do away with taxes. I just said the automatic withholding should go. It puts us to sleep. We don't pay attention until the end of the year and then we wait anxiously, like pathetic proles, hoping that Daddy Government will give us some money back. OUR MONEY!

Further, our tax system is a grand waste of money. The government spends billions making sure you pay your "fair share". Then it spends more refunding what turns out not to have been your fair share after all. Billions more are wasted chasing scofflaws that don't pay. And in the private sector, companies spend mountains of billions in compliance to tax laws. This is all money that comes out of your pocket and helps make the things you buy more expensive. Yes, your pockets. I am speaking to *you*, personally.

In fact, I'm looking at you right now. Creepy, huh?

There's a much more effective way of collecting taxes. More importantly, this tax will be there for us to consider every time we make an installment.

Do you remember when I said we should get

rid of all the goodies? One of those goodies is a tax refund. It is a joke to begin with. It demonstrates that the government shouldn't collect as much as it does. It is also an interest free loan to the government. If all we did on the personal income tax level was to make it payable on an annual basis, your TV and your google machine would be inundated with banks and credit unions touting their tax account plan. You set aside your monthly tax burden in an interest bearing account and at the end of the year; voila (that's French for "tah-dah!") you cut Uncle Stickyfingers a check. The interest is yours. The more imaginative institutions will even offer you the service of calculating your total tax liability and help file your return. Sweet right?

But there is still a question of all the money wasted by the government chasing money to begin with. So we are going to take it one step further.

Kill the Income Tax, and Initiate Point of Sale (POS) Retail Tax.[19]

The effective tax rate, the amount actually owed, for the vast majority of people, is lower than the amount paid to the government each year. This is especially evident, on 15 April, of people who claim zero on their W-4 hoping to get money back each year. (This particular approach to paying taxes is proof that we are brainwashed lemmings.)

Tax deductions are a combination of behavioral engineering and theater, designed to 1) get you to do something like buy a house or 2) convince you that you are "getting something" from the benevolent government. Both actually cost the American taxpayer money in compliance on the part of citizens and enforcement and bookkeeping on the part of the government. In other words, they are bullshit.

I know when I need to buy a house. I'm not going to make such a massive investment because Daddy Government will give me back a little *of my own money* each year for having done so. As far as I am concerned, I can buy my house and the government can BUTT OUT and charge me less in taxes to begin with.

To avoid all this, once we have slashed the government and put the balanced budget plan into effect, we can initiate federal retail sales or point-of-sale (POS)[20] tax. The POS tax would be unquestionably fair. But for now the government is too over bloated to be supported by even a 25% retail tax[21] which would be too high to charge people at the cash register. This, despite the $5 trillion+ that we spend in retail each year. It's scandalous! Criminal!

So radical cuts, some of which will be discussed later, must be made concurrent with the establishment of a POS tax. This will require a huge wave of conservative legislators and a gutsy president to pull it off.

There are two glaring advantages to the POS tax. There is the inherent simplicity. No more returns to file. No piles of paperwork to send to your accountant. The other is the fact that you will see the taxes you pay every time you make a purchase. Knowing the POS just added to the cost of your Big Gulp, you would be much more attuned to government waste and corruption. A tax on your big sugary drink to help those who can't help themselves? Maybe. But a tax on the same drink to subsidize the giants in the sugar industry? They can kiss your ass! Right?

An additional advantage to paying a POS tax: You will be paying a tax as a result of a voluntary action, not just because you committed the offense of being alive.

We all know that 15% of $1000 is the same burden proportionally, as 15% of $10,000 or $1,000,000. The vast majority of the media will try their Orwellian best to make you un-know this fact. They will pretend that making a successful person pay a greater *percentage* of his income than that paid by someone less successful is actually fair. That is ludicrous. It is that kind of twisted thinking that has allowed the federal government to become the monster it is today. It is the kind of logic that led to the ***earned income tax credit*** payable to people who have earned no income and paid no tax.

Voters and candidates alike should be prepared to slap down this stupid kind of argument at every opportunity. And the press will be stupid enough to provide lots of opportunities. In making your case, remind the listener their tax compliance will be wildly easier than it is right now and that each year, the government tax receipts will go further and further. This will be the result of more and more taxpayers working every year and the government pig being butchered down to a manageable, ethical and constitutionally correct size. And at no time will we have to remove the safety nets that exist for people below the poverty line right now. There may be people at 400% of the poverty line getting less than they get right now, but fewer of them will want it each year. They'll be making real income from real jobs.

Icing on the Cake

Here's another benefit of eliminating the corporate tax and creating the POS tax. Do you remember those board members and CEOs we discussed when talking about JC Penny and Home Depot? Well these guys spend incredible amounts of money on accountants to find ways of reducing their effective tax rate down to...well, zero if possible...but definitely lower than the prevailing bracket. It is all perfectly legal and I support a person paying the minimum the law allows. But they, like everyone else, will have to pay the going rate on what they purchase under a POS plan. And rich people buy really nice stuff! This will be a windfall in tax receipts. But if conservatives get both houses and the White House in '16 and hold on to them, the government won't have long to enjoy their new pile of money.

The net result is that it won't be necessary for the government to gouge the rich and the rest of us for 24, 28, 30% of our income. The neighborhood of 15% - 17%, maybe less, will do nicely.

Fair warning! The media, the Dems and the members of the establishment Republicans too stupid to understand what is happening this year, will fight this idea tooth and nail. This type of tax doesn't allow them to play games with tax money and cheat the American public. They will tell you that such a program will have terrible consequences. It will be fun to see how creative they get. But none of their protestations will be true. Write your representatives now and tell them to join the POS tax movement.

Now, dear reader, with some appreciation of where Uncle Stinker get his money, let's turn to how he might spend it more wisely.

6 GOOD STEWARDS: SWIMMING WITH SHARKS:

Government is not the solution to our problem. Government IS the problem.
- Ronald Reagan, 1981.
Who knew, in 2000, that "compassionate conservatism" meant bigger government, unrestricted government spending, government intrusion in personal matters, government ineptitude, and cronyism in disaster relief?
-    Christopher Buckley, 2008

On This, the Media Will Always Be Your Enemy

Gold is an element. If you could melt it down and pour it through a filter, what comes out the other side is gold. It can't be reduced down to something else. Put more correctly, it is irreducible. So must be our message if we are to win multiple elections.

We have seen time and time again, when discussing taxes and the economy, that the mainstream press, and not a small chunk of the alternative media, will look facts straight on and report something other than the facts. Whenever a Republican outlines a tax or spending bill, no matter what numbers are used, he will **always** be accused of favoring the rich.

So please candidates and handlers, don't distract yourself by trying to please the media, especially on such important issues as these. You will not be given a truthful minute of coverage. Instead, recognize that the media is a filter and will try block your message. Make a case strong enough and simple enough that the media will not be able to change its nature. Your message will leave the bullshit machine in basically the same state as it entered.

But don't try to tailor a message that you think the media will like and cover accordingly. They won't do that – ever! Not during the campaign. They eventually will, years after your plans meet with success, as they were forced to do with Reagan's economic juggernaut. And you are going to have success, right? Because you are going to have loooong coattails 22, right?

Reagan's plan was far too complex and not as strong as the options out there today. Despite this, we rode the Reagan wave from the early 80s until 2008. We weathered the damage the economy endured with Bill Clinton, 9/11, two wars and "compassionate conservatism"23.

What we need desperately in this economy is simplicity and clarity. The simplicity should be the easier sell for the vast majority of voters. Some will be skeptical because of a lifetime of being told that government programs must be complex. Only the governing class likes complexity. It allows the elites to build little empires around their programs to manage the endless minutiae that federal law excretes by the wagonload. For examples, look ad Dodd-Frank and Obamacare. Combined, they represent almost 40,000 pages of Orwellian untruth. The Financial "Reform" act was an intentional maze written to preserve the status quo among friends of Democrats, disguised as a bill to help consumers. All it did was make life more indecipherable for everyone and create thousands of careers in compliance and enforcement. Obamacare by itself is just shy of 30,000 pages of regulation. And as we all know by now Obamacare cannot and will not do anything for anyone except for the chosen few insurance companies *that wrote the goddamn bill!*

No more of this. We need ideas that people can get their heads around the first time you explain it to them. If you want to set the electorate on fire despite the fact that the press will lie about you and what you are planning, try simplicity and clarity. Make your message as elemental as gold.

The Budget

It is the clarity that will be the tougher sell. It is here that you make understanding your plans simple. But it is also here, that you make clear to the voter that what they *think* are goodies from Papa Government, are not goodies at all and are going away.

We'll start with the budget. The best plan proposed in the last two decades is what is called the Mack Penny Plan. It goes something like this:

You choose a recent year's spending level in which no one died due to the fact that the US Government was too small, say 2014. Whatever was the total spending for that year will be the total budget for the coming year. Next year you cut that by one percent across the board; one penny on the dollar. No exceptions. Then you do the same thing again the following year. This is repeated for 7 years. Each year, the one percent is, in actuality, a smaller number than the year before because it is one percent of a smaller total amount. The result, you have balanced the budget.

Liberals and our not-too-bright conservatives are already squirming in their chair with the first objection.

But MJ, that can't work, it's too simple! Nothing is that simple!

The Next Teachable Moment

Here the wise candidate gets a chance to outline his economic program by teaching the public some basic truths they probably already know to be true but have been convinced to *think* otherwise.

Why are liberals and RINOs so impressed with needless complexity? I can understand the governing class on this point because they believe in gathering power unto themselves and need byzantine barrels of regulation as mentioned above to hide their desires. But in conversation with people about this very point, a lot of otherwise smart people complain of the simplicity. Why would the regular Joe complain of simplicity when the optional complexity is a millstone around his neck? See it for what it is – a lifting of a great burden from your life.

Things are only as simple or complex as we insist on making them. Controlling spending and balancing budgets is not like sending a man to Mars. People and corporations do it every damn day! Expect the same from those in whom you have entrusted your hard-earned treasure. If you don't see the truth in this, put this book down now. You are too stupid to absorb the rest of it.

The trouble with any bureaucracy is that too many people, instead of doing their jobs, spend all their time building little empires and call that management. It is invariably a distraction from the primary mission. They HATE simplicity, especially when it comes to budget cuts. Broach the subject and the thousands of little empire builders in the federal labyrinth will be saying, *Oh no. That's fine for some other department, but my little corner of the world is far too valuable to absorb what will be approximately a six percent cut over seven years. Take more from this and that program, but give me my regular increase.* - OR - *Our workers are the finest workers in the entire universe (even the ones who look at porn all day) and we can't afford to layoff a single one of them. The federal worker is the very bedrock of*

Western Civilization.

I'll take those two examples of self-preservation, at the needless expense of the taxpayer, in order.

To defend little government empires - and we heard this with the sequestration arguments - the little emperors will cry, *by golly how can I plan next year's work if I have to cut everything by 1 percent? We have new programs going online. They must be paid for. If you are going to just willy-nilly cut one percent of my budget, we may as well shut down the whole department!*

Don't tempt us.

This was, at the time of "sequestration"24 and still is, a riotously specious argument. The operative word here is planning. So, in 2016, as an example, Congress acts responsibly and passes the budget for 2017. The budget provides all departments a pre-sequestration budget of X dollars minus one percent. Now, planning begins on how to incorporate the cut. As professional employees, the little emperors should be expected to meet this requirement. If they can't absorb a one percent cut, they should be fired and replaced by competent managers.

Also, if they were told they were getting an increase of any kind next year, as the federal government has gotten EVERY year for the last

40 years, they would have no trouble planning for that and spending every last dime.

As for the layoffs of government employees...

This is where the shit really gets deep. You would think every government employee was a snowflake with a degree from MIT. You'd think they all had 3.2 perfect children, had the work ethic of an Amish farmer and sang *God Bless America* every morning before starting work.

I'm here to tell you, after 23 years in the navy and 14 as a contract employee for the Department of Defense, the previous paragraph is beyond fantasy. There are some truly great people working for the government. I've had the honor to work with some of the best. But as an organization, I can tell you, being good stewards of public funds is not at the top of anyone's priority list. And there are thousands, many thousands of highly unproductive members of the federal workforce.

I can see the news stories now. Media hacks will search frantically for a story that will show an excruciating tragedy caused by a 1% cut in funding. We'll see the 22 year old that had just settled into his new job at the Department of the Interior, now the only layoff in the whole department, cast out into the cold. So unfair.

Or, among the proles, we'll see the face of a crying, single mother with five kids, from three different men, who can't make rent this month because her landlord demanded the extra $8. 00 the government didn't pay in housing assistance. Kids will be forced to walk around in New Balance instead of Nike, shattering their delicate self-esteem. Schools will be forced to serve food the kids will actually eat instead of the arugula Michelle Obama commanded them to eat. And don't get me started on the 1000 fewer welfare cell phones that won't go out this year.

Give me a minute. I'm tearing up just thinking about it.

That said, with one percent cuts per year, it isn't necessary to get rid of even this dead weight; at least not early on, and never in great numbers. If you cut payroll by one percent, EVERYONE'S new spending authorization by one percent and required that any new project be within budget and/or offset by curtailing other projects, the need for layoffs becomes very remote.

But there would be some. As you get further through the budget reduction plan there would have to be some reorganization. That's what the planning is for. Get rid of the dead weight first.

And speaking of dead weight, there is much

more we can do *in conjunction with* The Mack Penny Plan to reduce spending and take the first steps to shrinking the size and reach of the government. Remember, I said, "in conjunction with. " Even the smallest government operation could use the discipline of spending less. If they have to do less (1% less) that is likely a very good thing.

We'll talk about taking away the "goodies" and really shrinking government in a chapter that will give the weaker candidates a heart attack. One can only hope.

7 SWIMMING WITH SHARKS...WRIT LARGE

Back home we got a taxidermy man. He gonna have a heart attack when he see what I brung him!
- Quint, *Jaws,* 1975

Along with small cuts needed to balance the budget, there is an opportunity with this election to slash the executive branch, make the President's job easier and less smarmy, and save *multiple hundreds of billions* of additional taxpayer dollars. We also want to reign in the federal monster. In this book, I am suggesting that the next chief executive preside over the greatest surrender of power since George Washington turned his sword over to Congress.25 The executive branch needs to be heavily reduced and responsibility for making law must be put back on the shoulders of Congress; preferably one not presided over by the Four Morons of the American Political Apocalypse26. If you are reading this as a Congressional aspirant, you will want to assist this new President in returning power and relevance to the legislature. *Remember, legislators*; other than foreign affairs and the veto power, this man's job is to execute YOUR will! Hold him to account!

Voters, pay attention and insist this happens. Pound your Congressional delegation, no matter what their party, with phone calls and emails demanding that they put on the man pants and take back the power that is by law, theirs.

Everybody thinks that his rep is a great statesman. Every two years polls indicate that an overwhelming majority of Americans want to throw all the bums out. And every year more than 90% get reelected. Clearly, legislators go home with the same message year after year: *I'm the good guy. It's all the other guys who are ass hats.* Don't buy that. Check his voting record. Where does he make the most appearances?

Do you know what a legislator's most common complaint is? No letters, no phone calls from constituents. They often don't know how their people feel on many issues. SO LET THEM FRIGGIN KNOW! MAKE THEM EARN THEIR PAY! Don't worry so much about the rest of Congress; that's the concern of people in all the other states. Ask what the hell your delegation has done for you, or at least not *to you*, recently.

Then challenge his or her sense of adult responsibility...often!

Politicians be warned: If you are not a candidate in control of yourself or the facts, you would be better off quitting the race forthwith than to venture into these waters. If you are not a Fiorina or Jindal or Walker, you may suddenly find yourself being dismembered by the sharks in the media, the Beltway and by the citizenry that you failed to convince. Lindsay Graham; I like you. I always have. But you don't stand a snowball's chance in hell of being **this** guy. It's the same with Jeb Bush. If anyone shows the audacity required to push any proposal in this book, Jeb will be knocked to the middle of the pack. If Bush tried this right now, the sharks would tear him to pieces. Not because he couldn't do all these things, he can. But so far his campaign is too risk averse and business as usual to stand up to the onslaught that a less than ethical media would bring to bear.

But it is audacity that paves the way for massive victory, so I would hope that some of the conservatives take on at least a goodly portion of this chapter.

This Will Give Carl Rove a Stroke. Any

Takers?

Over the last two decades, we have seen spending, the budget and the national debt skyrocket. Even sequestration continued the growth. Hundreds of billions were added to our spending, again and again. When cuts would be touted, and there have been few, they weren't real cuts, just smaller increases.

Well, it's time. The people are prepared – make that starving - to hear that someone is about to take a broad axe to the federal monster. Here are just a few humble suggestions from your loyal servant.

Whiteboards ready? Summarize this section and start scribbling.

ELIMINATE THE DEPARTMENT OF EDUCATION!

Of all the departments I will take on, this one is the most useless by far. The Department of Education (ED)27 takes the blue ribbon in wasting taxpayers time and money. *No Child Left Behind! Common Core!* INDEED! The ED has never educated, nor has it contributed to the successful education of a single citizen of the Union. This is the most useless collection of bureaucrats ever assembled. Like *some* of their local and state counterparts, the ED exists to keep these people employed. They do nothing but add to the cost of educating our children by syphoning our tax dollars and making pronouncements that do not contribute to student success.

There is a legitimate explanation, of course. They know nothing. No desk warmer in DC knows the first thing about what your child needs to be successful. They claim to. Some actually think they are omniscient and can discern the perfect solution for every state, county and municipality in the country. Most of these delusional creatures are liberal doctrinaires and really, REALLY believe that Big Brother knows everything. Like their betters in the White House, these people read *Animal Farm* and *1984* and instead of being repulsed, sat back and thought: *This could work! I could be an important person in this world!*

The most important thing a candidate needs to know is that starting your cuts here will be like shooting fish in a barrel. Democrats will be apoplectic. The press will actually froth at the mouth. Government spokesmen will run to the nearest podium to tell us that every last employee at ED, and all the other departments we are going to eviscerate in this book, are the most indispensable people in the history of man.28

Weak Republicans will try to crawl under refrigerators to avoid talking about it. We will hear that dumping the Education Department will sound the death knell for western civilization.

Don't worry. Joe Sixpack and Lilly Minivan will hear you are closing down this monstrosity and do a Tiger Woods fist pump. And you, brave candidate, can rest easy. There are more Joes and Lillies in this country, black, white, Asian, Latino, gay, left-handed, *even on the federal payroll* than any other voting cohort. Go for it!

As for the invaluable qualities the typical federal employee might possess, let them put those qualities to the test by going forth and offering their services to the states and cities. If it is true that they are the best things since perforated toilet paper, they won't be unemployed for more than a week. I am being facetious, of course. But they shouldn't worry anyway. The economy we are going to spawn from this and other federal dismemberments will create so many jobs the average citizen will need to hide under his bed to avoid employment.

Reduce the IRS to a Bookkeeping Operation

There are many reasons to take the teeth out of the IRS. The most recent to come to light is that the organization has become little more than an attack dog for the governing class. Lois Lerner and that smirking, smug Koskinen are convinced that the American citizen is so thoroughly cowed that the IRS can do whatever it wishes to whomever they dislike. They share Obama and Hil-liar-y's view of a socialist utopia. They feel utterly at ease abusing you and your money and your personal liberties in order to tamp down political descent. This is the fault of the gutless wonders inside the Beltway right now, especially the four morons. Trey Gowdey seems to be doing something, but he is moving terribly slow. He ought to quit messing with his hair and get on with it.

No matter. As we saw in the chapter entitled "Other People's Money" the tax code can be made infinitely simpler than it is today. A point-of-sale tax will render the IRS obsolete. The only function of the new IRS will be to monitor the receipts of retail businesses. Those businesses will have little, if any, motivation to skirt the law for people they don't know. They will produce the revenues needed to run what will be left of the government, once it has been leashed and cut down to a manageable size. For those businesses stupid enough to lie about their monthly sales or companies that don't do their bookkeeping correctly, an IRS 1/100th its present size will be sufficient to roll those businesses up and close them down.

I can hear the non-thinkers nagging me again:

But MJ, what about all those poor out-of-work IRS agents?

First, lets acknowledge that these virtuous and invaluable public servants allowed, and in many cases, participated in the harassment of citizens who didn't agree with the sitting emperor. Few, if any, ever raised an eyebrow. So my heart isn't breaking at their dismissal. But once again, our own austerity will come to the rescue of even the undeserving.

Bust Medical Scammers...

One of the areas needing to be addressed is the obscene amount of fraud and waste occurring in government and by citizens raping the federal dole for entitlements which they are not, well, entitled to. The rate of fraud in Medicare alone is in the tens of billions per year;[29] $50 billion each year according to the government's own estimates. Some say it is closer to $80 billion.

To start addressing this, we transfer an army of those agents the IRS will free up to the

Department Of Health and Human Services with the same police powers they have right now. These agents will carry Department of Justice badges. They won't work for the agencies they monitor. Turn them lose on the fraudulent scum who are directly stealing our money. But with this caveat: in order to bust individuals, they must also take down any skanky, quack doctors that may have made their fraud doable. And such scum should do serious jail time!

Continuing on the medical fraud theme: Since the ugly, grey dawn of Obamacare, millions of people have illegally, if not understandably, left the workforce, applied for and gotten disability checks from the Social Security Administration. After being forced from the workforce and living in an economy with zero *real* growth for several years they gave up and took the bait being offered by Valerie Jarrett's lapdog. Obama is why people like Jarrett keep community organizers around. The easiest thing to do in this country is breath. The second easiest is to get on Social Security Disability. Hell, around the time Obamacare was being rolled out, the White House had people recruiting citizens to sign up.

More of these IRS agents, after years of serving the emperor, often willingly, can be sent to DHHS to warn off and, if necessary, bust those on disability who go to the gym more than my gainfully employed readers have time to. Agents can also go after those who collect a government check and work under the table.

But I'll say it again; the economy we are going to grow will pull people off the government dole. And since we will be heavily means testing this bloated program and drastically cut the rates for those who don't really deserve it, many of these people will leave their disability behind and get real jobs. For those who do not, they get one LOUD warning: if you are not sick, get off the dole. Leave it for those who need it.

... and then Cut Those Departments Accordingly.

There is an endless, sickening litany of people ripping off the government/us, both private citizens and government employees. You should be able to pull 90% of the IRS and transfer them to other areas to clean up the mess. Make these agents answerable to people outside the target organization they police, and transfer them often.

Fear alone will curtail billions and billions of dollars worth of waste and fraud.

Once you have reduced the fraud by tens of billions, cut that amount from DHHS. There is much more to be done to bring this department to heel, but you get the idea. I gave you a good start.

Eviscerate the EPA

Did you know the EPA packs heat? Oh, yeah. Nice stuff, too. SIG Sauer; stainless steel, no less. I own five weapons. I can't afford a stainless steel SIG.30

WTF?!?!

The EPA is a *policy* arm of the government. What jackass gave them police authority? How can it possibly be justified?

Let's suppose the EPA decided the drainage ditch in your backyard was a protected navigable waterway. *I'm not half kidding on this one; they do this kind of monkey shit all the time.* Once established, they can cite you for any one of dozens of things you might do to or near this *waterway.* Let's suppose further that you build a 10' x 12' storage shed you bought at Lowe's and plop it near this critical body of H2O. Should Big Brother find out about this, and find regulation against it, the fun would begin.

You would be cited, of course, and told to get the offending shed away from the life-affirming drainage ditch. If you refuse, then the fines and arrests come into play. There was a time when the EPA would have to notify the Justice Department and/or local police to assist in assaulting your property, tearing down your shed and dragging you into court. Now it seems they have the guns and police powers to do it themselves. Brilliant. What a time saver!

Along with police powers, these people now have the power to make laws. They say they are just expounding on proper law, debated and legislated. But as we have seen, through new "regulations" supported nowhere in existing law, they are *dictating* NEW law. We also know they have the blessing of an authoritarian regime to do it. "I can't wait for Congress..." and all that jazz.

One of my favorites is that CO_2 is now, by totalitarian fiat, a pollutant; a toxin; fucking poison! Who knew?

I was shocked to hear this. I immediately wrote my Congressman (He's the good one. It's all the others that are ass hats.) and demanded that a warrant be sworn out on every single American. I have it on good faith that several times a minute every single one of these damnable Americans is spewing carbon dioxide into the atmosphere. And they do it all day long, even at night when they sleep. They have absolutely no regard for their planet. Bastards!

It should be easy to catch them. The NSA has all their phone and computer records. They can pull every phone conversation these criminals are having, find out their movements, who they are talking to, and arrest them.

Taking it an important step further, do you have any idea how many tons of CO_2 are being expelled by *9 billion people everyday?* Oh yeah! The whole world is doing it. The trees have absorbed so much of the poison they're turning green!

We can't arrest the whole world. So Valerie Jarrett should order Barry to bomb every last one of them into dust. And he can start with those Lithuanians. Thick as thieves, those Lithuanians.

The one thing more stupid than the last four paragraphs is the CO_2 declaration they are making fun of.

But I'll tell you something even more stupid and truly frightening. The person now at the head of an organization with fiat power and guns is a liberal, environmentalist doctrinaire. She is a propagandist and GW/CC alarmist of the first order. She is totally beneath our trust.[31] I speak of Gina McCarthy, EPA Administrator.

Reduce the EPA to a monitoring group and give them four initials.32   All the states have their own version of the EPA. Many simply lift environmental law directly from the federal government and make it their own. Call the new federal activity something like Environmental Policy Monitoring Group (EPMG), responsible to the states for *assisting* them in maintaining a safe, clean environment and settling environmental disputes among the states.

But for Christ's sake, take away their police power, rescind all of their fiat pronouncements of the last 7 years and take away their GUNS! Nobody wants some sunken-chested Occupy Wall Street type carrying a gun. He'll probably just shoot himself in the foot – or someone else's foot.

Subsidies Schmubsidies!

There are literally millions of ways to cut the thousands of programs that must be cut for the federal government to function in a way even remotely sane. For example, **welfare** should be one, means-tested program providing the recipient with two cards. One would work in grocery stores and one in other retail stores. Purchases with these cards should be linked to specific UPCs that would not be attached to junk food, booze, cigarettes, etc. And they certainly shouldn't work in ATMs.

College loans...

...and grants should be jealously awarded. It wouldn't hurt the future of this country if they were limited to science, math, language and history. *I know, I know; someone will then insist that Militant Lithuanian Athletic Studies is a science.* And the federal government should get out of the school loan business altogether. Has Uncle Skidmark ever gotten involved in a business that he didn't totally cock up?

Crony Corn Squeaz'ins

Subsidies for **ethanol** should have never been created. The industry still won't discuss the impact of production on the environment, claiming that the slightest explanations would compromise proprietary secrets. Why the hell do they get a pass? They won't say how many gallons of fresh water it takes to make a gallon of their crap. Why the hell do they get a pass on that?

Their crap retains water. This is bad for your engine. It is why smart people put boat fuel in their lawn mowers. No ethanol. Ethanol would ruin them. Ethanol scorches cylinder walls.

The big reason to dump the crap is because it doesn't produce the performance per gallon that gasoline does. So having ethanol in your tank may cause a little less pollution out of your tail pipe *per gallon,* but it takes more gallons per commute, for example, thus producing more pollution per hour the car is run. So at best it is probably near a wash to go with it or without it, minus the consideration for engine damage.

There are independent experts who, if given access to the "proprietary information" the industry hides would likely prove all of this. But on its face, it makes perfect sense anyway. Ethanol is a waste of time and a standing insult to the American taxpayer. Flush the shit.

Note to the Republicans who fight every year to save the ethanol subsidy: You are whores who have abandoned the principles you claim with your party label. You must feel skanky when you fight this dishonorable battle every year. But hey, a lot of that taxpayer money comes rolling back your way every election year, doesn't it?

To farmers on the government corn dole: Just a few years ago, many of you were broccoli, wheat, peanut or whatever different kinds of farmers there are. By jumping on the government subsidy wagon and switching to corn, then selling it to the ethanol machine, you participated in an artificial rise in food and feed prices. I refer most directly to the big super farms operations. It *is* a free country and you were offered the whore money from the government. It is certainly *legal* to take it. But you can kiss all of our asses anyway.

The bottom line on ethanol is that without artificial sustainment from the government and the police state requirement that we put the crap in our gas tanks, there would be no one willing to buy it. That's because it is of no valuable use. If it provided great gas mileage or extended the life of your engine, everyone would buy it. But it doesn't. It's crap.

The list goes on. For the sake of simplicity, I will paint with a wider brush. But the light is starting to come on in your head. Whether you are a voter or a politician, you are starting to see the genesis of an earth-shattering message here. It will set you apart and make you the distraction from the rest of the news. There is no need for you to take all this and carbon copy it onto your campaign. Take the ideas and plug in things you know will work, but think big. Small ball is for losers.

And now you REALLY have to open your

mind to Madisonian thinking33;

An old idea brought new again. Hold on t'yer ass, Fred.

The federal government should do away with **all non-welfare subsidies**. **All**. That's right. I have never met a subsidy that I thought was worthwhile. In the eyes of those who cannot open their minds right now, that makes me a hater. People will say *just look at all the programs that the government supports out of sheer kindness. The government is acting as it should in subsidizing them.*

Uh, sorry, Dudley Do-right. No, the government is not. In providing subsidies, especially popular ones, the politicians are whoring themselves to gain votes. With others they are doing it nakedly for the money. They are outside their mandate, causing people to live their lives more and more for the interests of others and not their own.

Well, why not?, you might snidely sniff. *It would do people some good to take care of others and learn the value of charity. Or a person must recognize that helping oil companies find oil is good for everyone. Or if XYZ business fails, people will be laid off. They need the government money.* Blah, blah, blah.

First, I implore you to read *Economics in One Lesson* by Henry Hazlitt. This PDF file can be downloaded free from the Ludwig von Mises Institute. It explains the basic, timeless economic realities the world works under and goes into great detail about the stupidity of subsidies, especially subsidies for businesses. Any business that needs to depend on subsidies should be out of business. The fact is most of the companies taking subsidies don't need them. But they'd be crazy to pass them up so long as they are available.

Also, when the government takes from one and gives to another it does so under the color of authority and the threat of a gun. That is not charity. That is coercion.

And if you do the long division, as Henry Hazlitt has, subsidies benefit only the recipient of the subsidy. They **hurt everyone else**. What you don't pay for in full by yourself, at the time of sale, you end up paying full boat, along with the cost of someone else's portion, plus the government's cut for brokering the subsidy scam. It makes your life more expensive!

That's why, before the government was run by total retards, they didn't subsidize the buggy whip industry with the dawn of the automobile age. The people in that industry had to find other work. And they did, thanks to the newly disrupted and exploding economy. The buggy whip lost its usefulness...unless you like to dress in leather skivvies and say, "Yes mistress!" a lot. Erm...uh...ahem. Moving on...

But here is the real rub. If they do away with all subsidies, that means they'll take yours. Bad right? No. If you are a productive, taxpaying citizen it is a wash at worst. We may not get our mortgage write-off, but we will no longer be financing thousands of other things, born of crony capitalism, that we presently do not benefit from.

For example, the government has pissed away $154 billion of *your* money on "green" energy swindles34. The companies involved were usually tinker toy operations with no hope of generating energy on a large, dependable scale. Or they were phony scams intended to fail, while the top brass left with *your* money still in their pockets. That's more than $4000 wasted for every man, woman and child in this country. If the government decided to give that back to you in cash as opposed to the "green" scammers, how would that compare the few hundred dollars the average mortgage write-off would be. And that's just one program. They empty the coffers every year on stupid ideas and then borrow as much as we produce annually, as a nation, on top of that. EVERY YEAR!

How are all your write offs put together looking now, compared to that? We have been, year in and year out, strapped with greater and greater taxation and government debt while being convinced that the pittance we are left with in the form of a write-off is a *really good deal*. I have news for you. The house always wins. They take more than they leave and you don't get the benefits; at least not one equal to what has been taken, and certainly not if you are a productive citizen.

And as a bonus kick in the giblets, the government competes aggressively against its own citizens for every dime of credit available so it can waste our future money on what it can't pay for this year.

P. T. Barnum said there is a sucker born every minute. I can tell you where 310 million of them live. That's what I mean by *Swimming with Sharks Writ Large*. So many of our citizens actually believe the federal government is interested in their welfare. They will be spitting mad that we intend to take their "benefits" from them. We need to convince a plurality of Americans that their future relies on doing for themselves, not taking a miserly whore's tribute from a corrupt central government. Which of our band of merry conservatives has the sack (or sacklette) to take on this fight? If that candidate emerges, will you vote for him or her?

8 AND THE HITS JUST KEEP ON COMING!

"The only thing that saves us from the bureaucracy is its inefficiency. "
- Eugene McCarthy

"Bureaucracy is a giant mechanism operated by pygmies. "
- Honore de Balzac

We Seem to Train Our Unemployed Like We Train Syrian Rebels.

Did you know the federal government spends $18 billion per year on 47 "job training" programs? Did you also know that "almost all" of these programs, according to the Government Accountability Office, overlap each other in terms of function and purpose? Did you know with all but a few, there are no methods of telling if they resulted in even one person trained or one job acquired? Did you know the ones with a matrix to measure success haven't been tested in years?35 Did you know Obama, king of crony kingpins, proposed a new "job training" program in February of this year?

Similarly – we'll soon see how foreign policy is a reflection of domestic policy – we've been running training programs for Syrian rebels with a goal of fielding thousands this year. In a year and a half, we've trained **sixty!**

So here's a suggestion. Kill all the jobs training programs. They are big holes that we piss taxpayer money into.

When the opposition demands compromise, offer to have only one program. That program must have measurable results, reported quarterly, and must result each year in total incomes to participants, in the aggregate, larger than the job training programs annual budget. If they have a problem with those requirements, tell them what Cheney told Leahy.

I'll Reiterate the Subsidies Thing.

Earlier, I said we should do away with all subsidies. They are a waste of your money and rarely, if ever, accomplish what they are intended to accomplish. Business subsidies are the most egregious. In many cases, like farm subsidies, they go to giants in their industry who are doing quite nicely without them, thank you very much. Sometimes, to defend them, we are told that we'd pay more to do business without the subsidy from Uncle Stupid. This is a fallacy. Instead of buying our sugar outright, at the market value, we pay our taxes, some of that money goes to the sugar industry and I make up the difference when I buy sugar. What is left out of that explanation is the cut the government takes for brokering this worthless deal. All the government does is create an uninvited middleman to be paid. And federal employee paychecks are pretty posh. If the industry were left to fend for itself, we would still decide how much sugar we want. If we find the prices to high, we'd cut back on sugar or suffer. Prices would go up or down based on our decision to consume it.

Now, consider the billions of transactions occurring in this country every day. Is anyone reading this book naïve enough to think that a gaggle of DC bureaucrats are capable of making policy to control the amplitude of each transaction to the benefit of the collective? If you think that can be done without simply making a mess of things, slap yourself hard across the face right now!

All subsidies are a sop for one friend of a politician or another. Even the most high-minded efforts have results ranging from nothing on the harmless end (there are few of those) to driving costs through the roof (i.e. mortgage subsidies, education subsidies, college and K-12, corn subsidies, you name it). Show me a business or other private activity the government has put a finger to that didn't turn into a three-ring circle jerk.

Use Your Imagination.

The list of things that could be done away with is a target-rich environment for a good statesman. If Congress made it their mission to do away with 300 laws per year that served no purpose, or negatively disrupted the program they were supposed to help, they would be thousands of years at the job. That is not a joke. Whether you are dealing in cash subsidies or "help" in the form of regulation.

Make a headline this week. Pick a target, preferably one larger than $50 billion and say, "I WILL TAKE A MEAT CLEVER TO THE XYZ PROGRAM!" and then in 100 words or less explain why. If the press has loose stools and prints banner headlines about your heartlessness, your pole numbers will go up. If the press has a moment of honesty and recognizes your understanding of how things really work, your poll numbers will go up. But as a good statesman in any post, your cuts have to be of value to the citizens and followed up on in office.

9   ON GLOBAL WARMING

"I'm not a global warming believer.   I'm not a global warming denier.   I'm a global warming agnostic who believes instinctively that it can't be very good to pump lots of CO2 into the atmosphere but is equally convinced that those who presume to know exactly where that leads are talking through their hats. "
— Charles Krauthammer, *Things That Matter: Three Decades of Passions, Pastimes and Politics*
"There is nothing more anti-scientific than the very idea that science is settled, static, impervious to challenge. "
- Charles Krauthammer, 20 February 2014

Not since Scientology, has a scam of this magnitude been foisted on the world. I speak **not** of the theory. That is a little understood and inconsistent phenomenon, at best.   Still, there might be some "there" there. For many, global warming has the ring of social issue, one of the phony issues we should be disengaging from. It's easy to make that mistake considering all the propaganda surrounding it, generated by emotionalist and alarmists.

But if you consider the economic damage that would be inflicted by the daisies-in-the-sidewalk approach the left seems to favor, this becomes an economic issue of the first magnitude. Their response to what could be expected (not occurring yet) warming? Why, just destroy the coal industry and replace it with wind and solar power. *Then,* send billions – and over time – trillions to other countries so that they can develop clean energy alternatives. I will spare you the diatribe and let you read the details in my upcoming book about energy and economics, but I will state simply that this money will NOT be used in these countries to build wind farms. They have other, more pressing problems, as do we.

The scientist chiefly credited with the GW/CC theory used two different statistical methods concurrently to achieve the now-discredited "Hockey stick" graph. Using the same methods in that manner you can make your birthday arrive earlier and earlier, each year.36 But take away the hockey stick and you still have a gradual warming trend. Many contend that the trend has been in place since the last Ice Age. That is reasonable. But others say that we are creating an envelope of gasses that are causing the atmosphere to warm faster. There may be truth in this as well.

I have never heard anyone address the fact that, with or without these gasses, we are warming our atmosphere directly and radically by simply running everything. Have you ever wondered why, when seeing the day's weather reported, the temperatures in cities, even small ones, are several degrees warmer than outside the cities? Is it a bubble of carbon dioxide floating above the city causing this? Of course not!

This is the result of mechanically generated heat from cars, trucks, busses, generators, pumps, computers, AC exhaust, ovens, stoves, etc.; hundreds of thousands of sources per city. Add to that the concentration of humans. If you don't think that is an important heat source, count the number of times an empty room calls for the air conditioner to come on. Then send five people into the room for the day and see how many times it kicks on.

As our cities have grown, the temperatures in these locations have gone up. 37

The last two paragraphs are, by far, more settled science than anything offered by the global warming/climate change alarmists...ever! None of the predictions made in the last two decades have come to pass. The excuses offered for us not seeing the disasters we were told were coming are many. Some may even be true. But this is unknowable.

Let's get serious.

All that said, one can neither confirm nor deny GW/CC as a man-made **emergency** with the least certainty. Both sides have a difficult argument because clear conclusions cannot be drawn. We don't even know what the optimum temperature of the planet is. We don't know if we are moving toward it or away from it. The hurricanes generated in the tropics from Africa to the Americas will be few this year because, voila (there's that French word again), the water in that region is colder than expected.

There are comments you can make, as a candidate addressing the issue:

So far there is too little data to go on before committing trillions of dollars to developing countries. Just saying *man-made global warming caused Super Storm Sandy* does not make it so and is not justification for the economic hardship suggested.

If the science does become less murky and emotionally charged, there is no sense in the US raping its own economy if Russia, India and China do not go along *at the same time*. The US has made unbelievable strides since the 1970s in cleaning our air and water. That will continue because people have discovered that clean and efficient is more profitable. Let the East, Russia and Africa catch up.

People who say they can predict a .6 degrees change in temperature decades from now, as Obama is claiming, if we all switch to wind powered washing machines or solar powered toothbrushes, **are liars** (Note, again, no one saw the cold water in the tropics coming.)

Claims that global warming is the greatest "national security" threat of our time are the most cynical and insidious of all the lies told on the subject to date. They are also the stupidest.

This should pretty much put Martin O'Malley on Loser Street, where he belongs. 38

The global warming propagandists will lose their minds hearing this. GOOD! Their shrill cry will get you mileage. More important, the average, levelheaded American will respond positively to an honest, responsible message about a subject that has often been handled with great irresponsibility.

10 OBAMACARE AND OTHER MEDICAL FANTASIES

Seven hundred and sixteen billion dollars, funneled out of Medicare by President Obama. An obligation we have to our parents and grandparents is being sacrificed, all to pay for a new entitlement we didn't even ask for. The greatest threat to Medicare is Obamacare, and we're going to stop it.
– Paul Ryan

It's too bloody bad the four Morons spent the last four years standing in the way of the quoted objective above.

This should be a runaway success for Republicans. But keeping in mind my earlier complaint about message and guts, watch a typical loser candidate handle the issue. He will say it is *bad policy and bad for our people.* If asked what he would do, he'll say the *Republican legislators take very seriously their responsibility to see that the American people get the healthcare they need.*

No, No, NO! This has been the consistent Alan-Shepard-prayer approach to the issue. This is worse than lame because it uses the kind of empty political rhetoric we have already decided to dispense with FOREVER. More importantly, it repeatedly misses the golden opportunity for real conservatives to pound away at the opponent and the program.

Say what you are thinking at this point.

Obamacare has nothing, *nothing,* to do with healthcare. It is a statist scam to take over a sixth of the economy and reward politically friendly insurance companies with the keys to the system. They will bilk it in exchange for acting as government administrators. It has failed in every conceivable measure. (Repeat that whole paragraph for effect.)

We are going to completely eliminate Obamacare from the federal register.

The insurance industry will issue real insurance policies.

We will cap medical damages. They were not invented to destroy caregivers.

We will permit insurance companies to sell insurance nationally, across state borders. This will increase competition.

We will let them offer the coverage they are willing to offer in exchange for what the consumer is willing to pay.

We will encourage businesses to delink your insurance from your job. There is no logical connection there anyway. Keep it "portable" as people now like to say.

Time to teach. We'll assume you are giving a speech on Obamacare or the subject has come up in front of an audience. If you are smart you have your board and easel ready. If you know how to use electronic graphics and still be interesting, go for it.

Write "Ins. Co" on one side of the board and "YOU" on the other. Using basic scribbles, demonstrate the following:

Insurance is a bet. All insurance policies are bets. Your homeowners insurance company is betting that your house will not sustain a serious calamity and you are betting that it will. If your house burns down, you win and you get a lot of money to rebuild. Your life insurance is a bet. If you die within a predetermined time, you win. They all work that way and were designed to do so.

Medical insurance used to be that. Each month, based on the risk the insurance company was willing to take, you would ante up with your monthly bet payment. If you stayed healthy the money stayed there. And as designed, if you got catastrophically ill or injured, the company would pay out your winnings; sometimes to you, sometimes to your medical provider.

The bet started to change some years back. People would get a cold and not be able to pay their physician. Such things weren't covered by insurance because number one, they are not by nature catastrophic and two because it is not a bet. There is a 100% chance that you will get colds from time to time. The same it true for rashes. The same is true for your kids getting stitches. People started going to the press and the government saying that they were put behind on their bills because their kids got stitches or the flu or whatever. Oh, how sad! There ought to be a law!

Remember Henry Limpet! Wishes Do Come True!

Well, the government provided laws, lots of them, to force insurance companies to provide for *everything*. The more minutiae that got piled into policies, the more expensive the policies became. Medical savings accounts are a great idea, but with increasing premiums along with all the money the government takes from us every month, who's got a few hundred dollars to open one of those? Also, since the insurance companies were forced to try to control rates and at the same time pay out on so many sure-winner bets, they became *increasingly* strict on what they would and would not pay on. Co-pays and deductibles went up.

Obamacare only exacerbates the problems and the costs. We were told we would save money because of Obamacare. But that was a lie from the very first. The system is, **by design**, more costly to the end user and was known to be so even while Barry was promising savings.

Now, my darling constituents, how would you like to have plummeting insurance AND medical costs concurrently? How would you like to have the *opportunity* to stash some of what you would save in an account to pay for incidental medical bills keeping cost low? How about fewer increases on your insurance premiums?

By going back to the days when medical insurance was for major injuries and illness, by allowing more competition, by letting people shop their medical dollar to any physician, by not encouraging defensive medicine39, we will see our medical costs fall into the basement.

But what about the poor and the elderly, who will take care of them?

Here's the best part of all. Without even changing eligibility requirements (more on that later) we can save billions by radically streamlining forms and compliance, and changing the way we pay out for Medicare and Medicaid.

Presently, Medicare and Medicaid, two of the four most scammed government entitlements are run by massive bureaucracies. Money comes in, the government takes its cut for doing nothing else but handling the money and creating mountains of needless paperwork, and then it gets paid out to states for distribution, which also costs money.

To save on all this, we need first, to do better means testing. Punish fraud with gargantuan penalties. Scamming critical assistance programs should rank up there with murder and violent crime in terms of penalty. If we need help in nailing the vile pieces of shit that try it, we can call on many of the suddenly out-of-work IRS agents40 to sniff them out.

Next, we convert to a voucher system. All those enrolled get a card. This card works nowhere but at point of service medical offices and pharmacies. It can only purchase prescription drugs and non-elective procedures. The cards carry a fixed value per week, month, year...the time frame can be anything that works best. If you shop your card against best price and practice, it lasts longer. Dollar amounts roll over. So as you accrue money in the card you are more prepared for catastrophe. At that critical moment, if you've been on the system for a while and have not abused it, the government needs to spend less of this year's dollars to protect you and top off our card.

Again, this is not an ATM card. You can't use it for anything but medical care. Payment comes through a closed system and is made to the caregiver. It would be no more complicated to set up than a credit card arrangement at JC Penny.

Separate Medicare/Medicaid dollars from the general fund. It never should have become part of that to begin with. If you ever want to really know the motivation behind these programs, along with Social Security, Obamacare, etc., just remember it was made part of the general fund. The idea was to fatten government coffers *first!* The government knew it would have to tax its way to paying out on this money later. So delink this and other welfare programs from all other spending.

Finally, compliance requirements would be radically streamlined. Once a patient is enrolled and has a physician, medical records and administration should be living documents, added to as needed and simple by design. Multiple **billions** would be wrung from the system every year with just this change alone.

We will always have fraud. These programs are always going to be with us. But they can cost multiple tens, even hundreds of billions less each year by simply administering them efficiently, and more challenging, honestly. An honest Republican, and certainly a conservative, should have no hand in growing these programs by one more penny. To do so would help *no one* and hurt everyone.

11 ENERGY POLICY (Micro)

BUILD THE KEYSTONE FRIGGIN' PIPELINE!

12 MINIMUM WAGE – MINIMUM THINKING

I was going to pass this one up as a phony issue, much like the Chicken Little global warming routine. But, like GW/CC, the consequences of pursuing the progressive agenda on minimum wage will have harmful results; especially for the people progressives are pretending to help. This is how I approached the subject in a blog post on streetpolitics.us.

Perhaps in the follow-on book to be out during the general election, I'll pick apart opposing articles line by line. No great challenge. Better still, I might consider a short e-book devoted to the subject.

George Will once posited this question, that if by some miracle everyone's net worth and income *measured against purchasing power* were to triple overnight, would the howling about income disparity suddenly go away? The answer is, of course not. The reason is because pundits and politicians favored by the non-thinking class would point out the lower third on the income ladder are still the lower third, and therefore cannot afford the four bedroom, three bathroom lake house the middle third now can. And that isn't fair. *One should fold one's arms and stomp a foot when uttering that last sentence. Assume I've done that for you.*

Fortunately, the free market system does not address what is "fair" in terms of how big your bank account is, how much I get paid, how shiny and fast his car is. That is up to you, your upbringing and your decision-making. In the free market, and I would contend, in a truly civilized society, the citizens have the sense and the strength of character to live their lives without complaining about the possessions and success of another. All this may be aside from a compliment on the qualities of whatever it is that person has garnered. The compliment would be a simple pleasantry. The rest is none of our business. Further, we meddle with opportunities, and the methods of success of others, at our own peril.

This is axiomatic in the thinking of truly successful people; people who made their own way in the world without resorting to the insulting of, or interference in, the lives of others. *Wow, the heads of Occupy Wall Street fans are exploding all over the country right now. Most, despite the fact that many are members of the 1% they pretend to despise and privileged with a college education. Yet don't understand the first sentence of this paragraph. And those that do, know it's true but also know they'll never be able to apply their global warming degrees with such dangerous ideas still lurking in the minds of thinking people.*

How does this apply to the minimum wage? Let's go back to the politicians I've been insulting since chapter 1. They know that a large majority of people thinks it's okay to raise the minimum wage. They also know, but wouldn't dare mention, that few people actually have to work for what is presently the federal minimum wage. They also know a few more things.

I've got it! We help the poor by taxing the poor!

First, the sector of the economy for which this wage was introduced (never having a lasting impact on those it was intended to help) is the unskilled, entry level or supplementary income sector. Wait staff in mid to low quality restaurants, gas station attendants, unskilled construction labor (we used to call them go-fers), janitorial staff, etc. Because of the simplicity and often the flexibility of working in these sectors, these jobs were typically offered to teenagers to give them entree into the working world and teach them a work ethic. For others it was supplemental income. None of the jobs the minimum wage laws are aimed at were ever intended to be a livelihood and were not designed economically to be so. The fact that middle-aged people have crowded out entry-level kids at Wal-Mart is neither our, nor Wal-Mart's, fault.

These same pandering pols also know that the electorate is shamefully uninformed. The average voter is asked, "Do you think people at the bottom of the income ladder should have more money?" And the average voter says "Sure, why not?" If asked, "Should the government mandate what a person's wages should be?" You'd get a sneer, at best. The correct answer is, of course, what an employer and an employee agree on, in the exchange of time for money, is absolutely none of the government's business. And the legislation to meddle in such arrangements is a waste of time *and* money. But there are politicians in need of cover from real issues, so here we are again.

Will raised another great point in a Fox News appearance last year. Who will pay for this rise in the minimum wage? Well, by huge disproportion it will be the poor, of course. Who does the most business with those earning minimum wage? It isn't politicians. It's not the guy who drives a Jaguar. It's people who eat and shop as inexpensively as possible. They will finance the lion's share of this stupid idea. And only a mouth-breathing idiot really believes that hours and jobs won't be lost and prices increased at those very establishments to completely offset, the new wage.

*As a side note, both McDonalds and Wal-Mart already pay above the prevailing minimum wage in most cases. Not all their stores, of course, pay the proposed minimum wage to **new** employees.*

But most employees presently move past that $10 figure rather quickly.

Here's a cool result of coming up with the magic number of $10. 10/hr. to solve the woes of the downtrodden. The downtrodden get to remain so a bit longer, as employers will be less generous with promotions and raises for established employees. And another! This will incentivize some restaurants to finally employ technology that's been out there for years. Automated ordering. Wawa stores are kicking ass with it. In fact they have been able to hire **more** people to cover the growth in business, so automation might just be a wash in extremely well run businesses. *It won't matter though. Occupy Sissy Street-types will put on their $250 shabby chic outfits and urinate in front of any restaurant that tries it.*

This latest iteration of pretending to care about poor people is the brainchild, as it always is, of politicians who find themselves in a hole and in need of some handy misdirection. The present administration has been an abysmal failure on absolutely every front. Between blatant failure, to corruption, to deaths by the administration's ineptitude (Benghazi) or design (Fast and Furious), this is a White House in constant need of Occupy Wall Street-esque distractions. Follow any news stream from the beginning and you will find programs trumpeted, programs failed, then the "rich" attacked and/or the "poor" pandered to. It is so naked it is embarrassing to watch.

The CBO reports that the new wage mandate will cost a few million jobs; although there's a *negligible* chance no jobs would be lost. This is good news according to the White House. They say that a few million isn't too many people to worry about and it MIGHT be none! Last week they were saying that the 2.5 million jobs estimated to be destroyed by OBAMACARE will be an excellent opportunity for some of us to relax and get out of those jobs we're trapped in.41

Trumka Gets His Cut.

Unions love the minimum wage also. As soon as it goes into effect, mark my words, they will point to union employees and say, "Look at poor Charlie over there", doing a job he **never chose** to grow out of. "Poor fella is only making $2.00/hr. over minimum wage! That's a disgrace! He needs a raise. " The effect this has on the bank accounts of the pure-of-heart (mobbed up) union "leadership" will only be a happy coincidence.

More and more (but not nearly enough yet) people are realizing that the government is a standing insult in many ways, this being one of them. Whenever politicians/unions claim to be "helping the little guy", know with crystal clarity that the only people being helped are the governing class and their own incumbency and personal gain.

Those who we are told will benefit directly from an increase in the minimum wage will see their gains eaten away rather quickly as the entire economy floats to a corresponding position with respect to their **big** pay raise.

I know, I know. I say all these things because I am a hater. All fiscal conservatives are, right? If I had the wisdom to be found in a drum circle or Justin Beiber pajama party, I'd be totally on board with this minimum-thinking idea.

Remember, government that assumes it can decide your minimum wage can also decide your maximum wage. It's been tried. Read up on Nixon.

13 RACE

"I guess it all depends on whom you ask and when you ask. Race, I've learned, is in the eye of the beholder. "
— Raquel Cepeda, *Bird of Paradise: How I Became Latina*
"Hockey is a sport for white men. Basketball is a sport for black men. Golf is a sport for white men dressed like black pimps. "
— Tiger Woods

I cannot believe the kid gloves we use to handle this subject. Please, someone remind me, are we actually stuck in a 1970's Movie of the Week? Is life now a never-ending episode of *Room 222?* Please!

There is one, and only one, correct approach a politician can take on the issue of someone's race. I DON'T CARE! No matter what office you might be running for, you need to make it 100% clear that you don't care what color a citizen is, or what ethnic group their parents hail from.[42] And I don't mean that you don't care in the tolerant, color-blind, sweetness and light sense. I mean you don't give a crap either way. Besides, what adult wants to be "tolerated" anyway?

In the Wrap Up, I will discuss the rhetorical power curve. But in the case of race in American politics we have utterly surrendered to the rhetoric of the left; the extreme crybaby left. The result is Republicans are left to sound like babbling idiots – "some of my best friends are black / Latino / Asian / Lithuanian. " Every week some lowlife Democrat throws the race card and like idiots Republicans line up to talk about how important, whatever flavor of race we're talking about, is to the very fiber of this country. We hear that we must work harder to "include" people of all races in the GOP and what a poor job we've done to date.

Guess what guys, whatever the race in question, black, Asian, Latino, isn't buying this stuff. And the activists are just recording the endless apologies to use next week when they call you racists again.

Stop defending yourself! The response to charges of racism is, "I don't care about race". If I am the dogcatcher, and I pander to any race, all others will assume that I have a bias toward that race. When I tell a race I *really, really* care about them because of their race, especially if it is different than my own, they know I am pandering, which is to say, they now know for certain that I am a racist. So if you come to my pound in search of your lost dog, as your dogcatcher I'm going to help you find your dog. I will do it because you are a citizen that my office serves. I don't care what race you are. It's not my job to give a rip about your race. If that troubles you, vote for someone who is racist and thinks you need to be coddled because you belong to a group that can't function like other races. If you want me to care about your race, you'll be sadly disappointed.

This attitude should spread through all localities and offices all the way to Washington DC.

Recent History

Several police units respond to reports of a man selling "loosies" on the street in New York. When they arrive they find an overweight, middle-aged man selling (gasp) untaxed and unregulated cigarettes.

Well, a cop might say to himself, *we're here*

and we didn't get all dressed up for nothin'. So I suppose if he won't give up his stash and move along, we'll have to take him in.

So far, I'm okay with it. They could probably be busting bigger fish, but they *are* here. But the takedown, in this case, resulted in a man's death! Yeah, I have to throw the bullshit flag on that one. Loosies don't rise to a level of strangulation.

Of the man's race, **honest politicians** should say what they were thinking when they saw the video; I don't give a red-hot damn. I wouldn't care if he was white, black, Latino (do you remember when the only acceptable PC term was Chicano?) or Asian. He was a citizen. You don't choke out a citizen in a takedown for selling loosies! Especially if he says repeatedly, "I can't breath!" *If he were Lithuanian...? Meh... Well, nah. You don't strangle Lithuanians either.*

Some people this week are cheering the Clinton woman for disingenuously pandering to them with her "black lives matter" remark. She is, by far, the least sincere politician in the United States. The listener should resent such blather. Her speechwriters put that line in there because it was trending on BuzzFeed. Only weak, self-centered people actually want to be spoken to in such a patronizing way.

If you live long enough, you get to see just

about everything. We got to see O'Malley embarrass himself with a phony apology for saying that *all* lives matter. If you favor the meme of the month, that black lives or the lives of any demographic matter more than another, then you are another person who should put this book down. You are too far-gone to make good use of the information to be found here. So drop the book and go away.

Institutional Racism

There are only a few places where institutional racism survives today. There is the KKK, the Arian Brotherhood, the New Black Panthers, La Raza; any institution that uses quotas in hiring, admission or advancement, and anywhere Al Sharpton is standing and not being arrested for tax evasion. That last one is a two-fer.

In the rest of society we have two obvious types of individual racists. The mouth-breathers often portrayed as Billy Bobs, believe that God created the world for white people. They think that when races intermarry, they are actually damaging the gene pool, though they have nary a clue as to what the gene pool is. Until recent decades they uniformly identified with the Democratic Party. I'd like to send the ones that became Republicans back.

The power hungry racists are the ones who insist that certain races cannot make their way in this world and must be controlled and conditioned to accept the "assistance" of their betters. This is true from Margaret Sanger, through FDR, to HRC. These people, who consider themselves superior over the races to which they pander, are enabled by the Sharptons of all races, who make their money telling people they have no hope.

Okay, I know there are some of you saying I shouldn't just use mob rat number 7 in so many examples. And you are right. I could have just as easily gone with, "the David Dukes of all races." Duke reemerged from the slime over the last couple of years trying to make anti-Semites out of our young people when Israel was stomping the scumbags that destroyed Gaza and rocketed Israel. He calls himself Dr. David Duke now. That gets funnier and funnier every time I hear it. Google him. One might fairly suspect he doesn't like Palestinians any more than he likes Jews or black people.

There is still another kind of racist. These folks consider themselves the most benign. They don't even know they are racists. And they are everywhere. These are the ones trying to catalog racial firsts. I contend they are just as detrimental as any other racist because they maintain the myth of *other.* Happily, they have pretty much outlasted they're usefulness. We have minority astronauts. A woman has held two of the most powerful offices in the United States, National Security Advisor and Secretary of State. And she was black. An Asian man heads the Treasury. We have the first totalitarian community organizer in the oval office. Jamaica sent a bobsled team to the Winter Games! There are no more racial firsts worth speaking of...with the possible exception of the first Laotian to head up the NAACP.

Teaching time!

It is one thing for a conservative candidate to say, "Well, Jeepers. We welcome all races to our party. " But the candidate who diminishes the significance of demographics in this country is the one who inspires people across the spectrum to ***want to be a part of this movement.*** And you won't inspire anyone by whimpering and apologizing.

I'll take you one better. Steal the next two paragraphs. Use them whenever you want without attribution.

I am running a campaign around critical

issues that face all of us. If you invite me, a candidate for federal office, to your town, house of worship, school, factory, don't expect me to address issues of race, class, gender, or shoe size. I will only talk about the economy, the federal budget, national security, interstate trade, and **getting the federal government the hell out of your way** so you can have a better life.

If you are a person who feels the need to treat certain Americans differently, **for good or for ill,** based on race, sex, religion or how many successive consonants are in their last name, please see your way to the extreme left wing of the Democratic party. We have no room for you in this movement. And as history shows, it is among socialists and totalitarians that racists are always the most comfortable and the most successful.

14 FOREIGN POLICY:

Hand Me Down My Foil Hat. Conspiracies Abound.

"[. . .] the foreign policy of any government [. . .] is a prolongation of its domestic policy. This is all too often forgotten in a period of 'summit' meetings, when the public is led to believe that three or four Big Men solve, or fail to solve, the world's predicaments according to whether they have or do not have the wisdom, the good will, or the magic wand needed for their task. "
- Isaac Deutscher, *Great Contest: Russia and the West*

When I look at the quote above, I realize that Obama has pursued a foreign policy that reflects just what Deutscher is saying. Our present stance in the world reflects Obama's naive domestic policy. This is a policy that says brilliant people can "manage" affairs infinitely larger than themselves. It also reflects the attitude that Obama has carried since childhood; that the United States is stronger than other countries and must be punished for that fact and reduced in stature.

It has been said by the religiously inclined that the biggest trick the devil ever pulled off was to make people think he didn't exist. It allows him to run wild and wreak havoc unchecked. Unaware of the source of evil, people can't stop him.

Similarly, the greatest ally of a corrupt government is the conspiracy theorist. Often labeled conspiracy freaks, these folks – if they are not too nutty in their appearance – tend to grab some headlines at first. If their complaints don't pass the smell test, they quickly fade from the public forum. The more outrageous and easily dismissed, the quicker that happens, and the moniker "freak" is assigned. This is often well deserved. The most egregious that comes immediately to mind is the 9/11 video of the twin towers with the second 767 digitally removed. The viewer sees a whole shaped like and aircraft suddenly appear, for no apparent reason, in the side of the building, **_followed by_** a fiery explosion. It was quite an effort to promote a silly argument, but sociopaths are often determined people.

The problem with having these freaks gaining press is that when real criticism gets too uncomfortable, we can simply label the speaker a conspiracy freak, or in some way nuts, and feel good about ignoring their complaint. GW/CC alarmists do it all the time. There is a book floating around out there that says skeptics just can't accept the GW/CC doom and gloom. You see, we're suffering from PTSD at the news that the climate is in such danger and therefore the skeptics are a bit crazy. Also, the *thing* that heads the EPA says that we are not normal. [43]

And that is where the real trick lies. In the case of our current government, we have been played for idiots time and time again because when confronted with serious charges, the target would either treat the story as a conspiracy theory or come right out and label the herald a freak. From Fast and Furious to Mrs. William Jefferson Clinton's emails, legitimate charges have been thwarted by thin straw man arguments and amused dismissal. White House press skank, Josh Earnest does this every single day. And he gets lots of practice because this administration is by far the most corrupt, totalitarian cabal in our history. Earnest doesn't spin from that podium; he lies from behind a smirk that is utterly contemptuous of criticism or honest discourse. And our pathetic media...they simply record the moment and go for cocktails. The few who do challenge the administration will only go so far for fear of loosing their press passes to the fetid sewer our executive mansion has become. They are not digging for information, nor for that matter reporting what is occurring right in front of them.

Uh-oh! Hilary Had an Oopsie or Ten.

Just look at Mrs. Clinton's email scam. She erased them. She said so. Her staff said so. The State department said so. The explanations were so childish, so breathtakingly disingenuous that one is left yelling the questions at the TV the press should be asking. Among the questions would be: What charges will the former Secretary be facing? What would the likely sentence be if she were found guilty? What about her lying to Congress about Benghazi (the US **was indeed** running guns to Syria via Turkey, as it turns out, to the wrong people)? So you can tack on real-world incompetence to homicidal incompetence.

Of course, such questions about that woman being charged with anything would be met with the freak treatment mentioned above – and most of the media would go along with it.

But when the truth is this obvious, a sycophantic press is not the problem. We are. It's easy to dismiss unpleasantness with dismissive labels, but in the case of this government, it is perilous to do so. We need to stand up. We need to deal with what has happened and *is* happening to our country.

But the above complaints are all prologue.

The most immediate priority is relieving Obama of any dealings with Iran. We have watched idly as he lied about his intentions to deal with their nuclear program. The entire three-year production has been a lie. When the administration said at the beginning of negotiations that Iran was 7-10 years from breakout (that point at which they could weaponize nukes) every literate human being knew it was a lie. And yet, when he said he intended to prevent them from attaining a nuke, the press pretended to believe that too. Late last year, a year and a half into the process, the breakout point was 12 – 18 months (hmmm, common core math?). Still a lie, and we were already lifting sanctions!!!! This year, when Congress said they wouldn't allow Obama to enact an agreement on his own the American Emperor said it is silly, at this point, to quibble. Iran was only about a month from breakout so we need to have this agreement to keep the genie in the bottle for ten more years! And besides, *it isn't a treaty,* they say, *it is an executive agreement.* No point in taking up the Congress' time with such paltry matters. News flash: Nothing will stop Iran from weaponizing; certainly not this treaty/agreement. **That was never the point.** More on this later.

And while witnessing lie after lie, what did Boehner and McConnell do? They "compromised" with Obama in the way in which they would be "allowed" to review this worthless, sham document.

Here are the two greatest offenses. One, McConnell and Boehner are the loyal opposition representing a separate and equal branch of a constitutional government. They do not work for the White House. Their job is to marshal votes for their position and issue orders, in the form of bills, to the White House. Such orders can be vetoed and that veto possibly overridden, but the bills carry the weight of the American will. Yet these two ineffectual idiots ask for allowances rather than insisting on doing their duty. In behaving this way all through these years, they have facilitated offense number two.

Here, I stand corrected on the piece I wrote in PP&E at streetpolitics.us about losing Egypt. I allowed for cowardice and incompetence as the reason for the United States losing our influence in the Middle East and North Africa. Sadly, there seems to be a more devious reason. Obama is not and has not been working to protect the interests of the United States abroad. Quite to the contrary, he has been actively seeking the advantage of a few Muslim countries **over ours**.

Look how far the administration has perverted its original stance on Iran, as an example. We have been watching the White house lobbying Congress, directly and through the press. They worked *strenuously* to protect an agreement that provides this country with absolutely no satisfaction while **facilitating** the production of nuclear weapons by the phony religious nut bags in Iran.

Don't take my word for it. Take any news feed from 2009 forward. Watch the pattern develop. From their starting point, Obama has steadily backed away from the original plan of complete prevention of Iranian nukes and possible regime change to accomplish that goal. From the very start the administration fought against sanctions. Throughout the process, they nagged Congress to lessen and then lift sanctions. While the Kabuki Theater they called negotiations played out and sanctions were reduced, Iran became more bellicose. They were downright cocky. They were clearly told that Obama was in their corner, not in ours. "Negotiators" would meet in plush surroundings in Geneva and go on record with phony positions, none of which were intended to go on paper in any real way. And as Iran raced to improve their nuke program, the Administration dug in its heels – *against the United States Congress!*

And elsewhere...

And it gets worse my friends, much worse. Question: If Obama really wanted to keep Iraq stable and not make a mockery of the loss of American lives there, why would he have waited until 30 days before the expiration of the Status of Forces Agreement (SOFA) to do anything to maintain our interests? And when he finally decided to act, why did he send Joe "Duh" Biden to do the heavy lifting? My previous answer in a PP&E blog allowed for stupidity. I now repudiate that assertion for one much clearer.

Barack Obama, Commander in Chief of our Armed Forces, the Chief Executive for the government of these United States, fully intended to leave behind a power vacuum for his friends from Iran to fill. The same Obama *wants* the vilest of Muslim countries to have a nuke.

The same Barack Hussein Obama *fought the United States Senate* in his attempt to preserve the power of the Muslim Brotherhood in Egypt. Fortunately for the citizens of Egypt, better people, who don't think religious nut baggery makes for good governance prevailed and ousted the nut bags, **despite the assistance** provided to the MB by Obama.

The insanity continues. Obama knew he couldn't just walk away from Afghanistan. But even with the "surge", a lame pretense of force costing American lives, Obama made it nakedly clear to those he favors there, that they should just sit tight, we'll be gone soon. Hell, he announces every withdrawal with each strategic adjustment.

And those who know better, Republican and Democrat have allowed this to happen. Whether watching the cabal gather power unto itself domestically with Obamacare and illegal immigration activity, or allowing the cabal to ignore the law in the cases of Fast and Furious, the IRS scandal, Bill's wife and her emails; those senators and Congressmen have done the United States and their own institutions a grave disservice. And they have compounded that immeasurably by allowing the President to sell us out to the power mongers in countries like Iran.

As I write this, I feel like one of those guys who puts tin foil in his hat to avoid government mind control. Yet, the information is there. The behavior has been consistent from Libya to Iran, from Fast and Furious to inciting riots in Ferguson and Baltimore. This is a President on a mission to be the guy who gave the US its comeuppance.

The common retort in the face of anyone accusing the administration of duplicitousness or vacillation is the phony, "Well what is the other option, WAR?"

The press has consistently failed to hold this nonsense up for the ridicule it deserves.[44] In the case of Iranian nukes, for example, there are many options. The most obvious was to maintain sanctions through negotiations and through compliance. It was the sanctions that got them to the table. As soon as the parties sat down, Obama started his push to lift the sanctions. The results are as stated above.

I am sorry to say that the next President faces the Middle East, North Africa, Ukraine, Iran and China with one hand tied behind his back. The present occupant of the White House has put us in a position far weaker than it should be. Whatever a conservative President might decide to do about these things and about our relationship with the rest of the world, he will have to do on his own. Our allies will not come along until they are sure we mean business and are already getting results. In other words, until we rebuild the trust Obama squandered. Our enemies will continue to thwart our interests to the same extent.

So prepare yourselves, candidates. When you step up and call all this international failure for what it is, you will be labeled a nut, saber rattler, a warmonger. If you agree with me you can only be legitimately called a sanctions monger, but no matter.

Stand tough. It is the only thing the voter and the rest of the world understand. The progressives and the media will have to be shown.

15 NATONAL SECURITY:

I'll Take Real Security, Please, With a Side Order of Personal Liberty.

"What is it that all these wage-earners, skilled artisans, soldiers and tillers of the soil require, deserve, and may be led to demand? Is it not a fair chance to make a home, to reap the fruits of their toil, to cherish their wives, to bring up their children in a decent manner and to dwell in peace and safety, without fear or bullying or monstrous burdens or exploitations, however this may be imposed upon them? That is their heart's desire. That is what we mean to win for them. "
– Winston Churchill[45]

If You Have Nothing to Hide, You Have Nothing to Fear.
- National Security Agency[46]

Knee-jerk jerks

During the post-9/11 debates that gave birth to what would be the *Patriot Act* and the Department of Homeland Security (DHS), I recall seeing a Senator, I forget who, exclaiming that Congress needed to pass something because, "we need to look like we are doing something!" This was in response to pushback from the White House, not wanting to create a bureaucracy in response to a violent attack. There was not one comment on CNN or FOX. I never read anything later about it in any magazine. Not even on Drudge. This comment was made from the well of the Senate!

What a breathtakingly stupid thing to say! How much more stupid were we? We stood like idiots and watched the 535 incompetents hatch two deformities that would only be outdone by Obamacare. Because they wanted to look like they were "doing something". In short order, Bush caved to the we-need-mommy-to-fix-everything fever on Capitol Hill.

First there was the *Patriot Act*, formally introduced in the House by Frank J. "Jim"

Sensenbrenner in October of 2001. It was a homogenization of the *Uniting and Strengthening America Act, Financial Anti-Terrorism Act* and a stampede of panic-button notions and whims floating around inside the Beltway after 9/11[47]. It was a massive decision, taken in haste by people who, as usual, **didn't read the goddamn bill.** Did it really need to address the Telemarketing and Consumer Fraud and Abuse Prevention Act? *Really?*

Despite Sensenbrenner's repeated insistence to the contrary, the NSA, the Justice Department, the White House and a Department to be named later noticed that the *Patriot Act* mentions wiretap, tracing and the FISA court (now a rubber stamp for anyone wanting to nose around in your phone records). They decided that it was the will of Congress that the NSA should take a vacuum cleaner to the Internet and phone records. They would process warrants that included such specifics as - everybody that Verizon has on record.

Boy, These Guys Have ALL the Answers...Just Not the Right Ones.

Fast on the heels of the *Patriot Act* was the creation of the Department of Homeland Security. Being herded like cattle through an airport, by under-qualified security guards[48] is only the tip of the iceberg for this monstrosity. And it is emblematic DC thinking.

In the 1970s the Israelis figured out it was a good idea to nail the cockpit door shut in commercial airliners. Their hijacking rate dropped to nil.

How did we deal with hijackings? Meh.

Long before subhuman religious nut bags flew planes into the Twin Towers, Tom Clancy released a book in which a Japanese pilot flies a 747 into the Capitol Building (1994). It was quite a shocker. But I remember thinking how easy it would be to do something like that. I wondered then, what we were doing to prevent such a thing. As Tom Clancy was one of the most popular authors at the time, it is a lead-pipe cinch that people in a position to know about these things also read it.

Reaction? Zilch!

In 1995, intelligence people in the *Philippines (!!!)* warned us that known or suspected Al Qaeda members were taking flying lessons in the United States. There would be several more reports of this kind of activity over the next several years. Including flying instructors mentioning how strange it was that the religious nut bags didn't want to learn how to take off and land; just how to maneuver in flight.

Still, no alarm bells.

By mid-2001 the FBI was just getting around to checking out some of the reports. They would later say that they knew that the subhumans were taking flight lessons but figured they were just planning for conventional hijackings, not a suicide mission.[49] (WTF?!?!)

Following the 9/11 attacks and the revelations above, did the government get serious and drill down into the existing intelligence and law-enforcement communities to route out the points of failure? Did they arrest, fire or even demote those who allowed the attack to take place through incompetence or indifference? Did they kick ass and make basic philosophical changes to the way these communities did business?

Noooo! That would have made sense. No, what the Beltway stooges did was create a whole new, cumbersome and equally incompetent bureaucracy to heap on top of the existing dog pile. Not only did they not correct the basic problems within the communities, they made their management and cooperation infinitely more complex. Even the very top of the chain of command for intelligence is now a Byzantine balloon knot of overlapping responsibility.

So, why the History Lesson?

So far, the only serious candidate to speak plainly about the mind-blowing incompetence on *all* levels of the government is Carly Fiorina.[50] She is also one of a handful of hopefuls who has the background to take on a large, philosophically malfunctioning loony bin that is our government and turn it into something to be proud of. Sadly, she is a big fan of mass data sweeping. Rand Paul has no equal in taking on the derelict DHS system and I believe he has the intelligence to be a superior President, but he needs to get real specific about his views and intentions if he is going to overcome his lack of executive experience as an image issue.

I go on a lot about how we need to shitcan programs that are the darling of the left cheek of the governing class. But the next POTUS must be willing to kill stupid wherever it rears its head.

Cleaning up the *Patriot Act* and fixing (eliminating?) DHS will be a tough fight. It is popular with both the military hawks and left wing statists. That alone proves me right on its overall worthlessness. But you will need the support of the public to deal with these pigs. Right now, all a commentator has to say is, "Well, what if we get attacked again? Then where will we be?" The public is presently convinced that DHS has been effective.

Please note that all or nearly all the terrorism busts have come from tips. These tips were from foreign countries or regular civilians who saw or heard something. The data sweeps have not produced one bust. The shoe bomber, the underwear bomber, the printer cartridge bombs all made it onto airplanes.

A fat, religious, nut bag on staff at Walter Reed Army Medical Center, communicating with known terrorists, was transferred to Ft. Hood where he killed 31 people shouting "Allahu Akbar".

In fact, Nidal Hassan was a major in the U. S. Army. He was responsible for the psychological wellbeing of American soldiers. And no one twigged to the fact that he was in communications with known terrorists. This, even after he would inject stupid, religious, anti-American rants into what were supposed to be meetings about military medicine.

Good job, NSA! Good job all you guys who worked with Hassan! Our special thanks go to his superiors for their timely action! You guys really know what to do. Like the national security posters say: *If you see something, keep your mouth shut or you might offend a fat, religious nut bag.*

Since 9/11 people have confused the terms *security* and *safety.* One of the few legitimate functions of the central government is to provide for the national security. They cannot provide for your safety. There isn't enough government for that. So if you are walking through a mall or boarding a plane thinking that the DHS is on the job and has your back, think again.

In the first paragraph, under the heading quoted at the beginning of this chapter, the NSA says: "Our value is founded on a unique and deep understanding of risks, vulnerabilities, mitigations, and threats. Domestic Surveillance plays a vital role in our national security by using advanced data mining systems to 'connect the dots' to identify suspicious patterns. " Well, the NSA, the CIA and the FBI had pretty good stuff before 9/11. The NSA is always decades ahead of the rest of us in terms of technology. But they couldn't connect the dots between a very realistic and popular story line and years of low-tech tips about terrorists right here in the US. They blew it then and they aren't much better at it now.

Don't get me wrong. If something were to happen, say a bomber using what looks like a box of Cap'n Crunch and a FitBit as a triggering device, blew up a comic book convention and you got whacked, you can rest assured the NSA would then collect all the data ATT had available on the guy. DHS would then make new policies to look for shooters or bombers that fit your killer's profile. We'd never see another box of cereal or an electronic wristband on an airliner or in a mall again! So there!

But since we'll not likely get a match on that again, the NSA and DHS will be left to react to the next killing – after the fact. But hey, be thankful there is a whole cabinet level department devoted to following up on one killing after another.

It is possible that, some day, a weird phone conversation will be picked up at precisely the right moment and a major, professional terrorist plot will be foiled. But you can't build a strategy on that. And such odds are not a valid reason to dig into the personal lives of every citizen.

Whether you are a private citizen or an aspirant to higher office, you have to look this stuff hard in the face. The DHS was an elaborate and expensive piece of theater designed to make you think the politicians were at the switch after 9/11, even though they weren't there one second before. Its creation has also added deleterious red tape to the already over-bloated law enforcement and intelligence communities.

One of the keys to good intelligence collection and analysis is knowing what you don't need as well as what you do need. Too much information muddies the process. Massive NSA data sweeps have one, and only one, purpose. To collect and store as much information as is humanly possible on *everyone* for future use. It will be used to either find interesting facts about killers after they have killed, or for powerful politicians to destroy you and/or your character if you make life inconvenient for them. *There is no other use for it all.* In order for collected data to be timely and actionable it would have to be much more discreet and come in much smaller, focused packages.

So my challenge to candidates and handlers is to talk to experts in the field. Avoid government lackeys. Honest experts can verify what I am saying. Continue your elementary school civics lesson, teaching people the value privacy holds for *them.* Teach them the potential costs of losing that privacy.

DHS as a Totalitarian Tool

We can go a step further. Why does the DHS have urban assault vehicles and billions of round of ammunition? All types of ammunition? In the event of war, agents from the DHS are not going to be loaded onto C-17s and sent to the front.

How might history answer this question for us?

Well, in the early 1930s, FDR was busy prolonging the Great Depression by making lots of busy work programs along with other statist policies to grow the size of the federal government. One of the programs was the Civil Conservation Corps (CCC). This was a national organization of (mostly) men, formed into military-style organizations and shipped hither and yon to build dining halls and walking paths through our national parks. It oozed national pride and propaganda. If you visit the Gulf Islands National Seashore (National Park) in Ocean Springs, Mississippi, you can walk on the remnants of one of these paths. At the turn-around, you'll see a faded photograph of the CCC on display. It is a picture of morning muster. The men are formed up, in uniform, in platoon-sized groups.

For Ma and Pa Kettle, the explanation for having a CCC was that men needed work and the national parks needed roads and paths, so we created the CCC. But that was not the main reason for its inception.

After the Treaty of Versailles was signed in 1919, French general, Marshall Ferdinand Foch echoed the misgivings of many when he said the treaty didn't bring peace but "an armistice of 20 years...no more than a 20 year truce. "

Everyone, with the possible exception of Woodrow Wilson, knew that another major clash of nations was an absolute. And most countries went about preparing for it. By Roosevelt's lights, as it was with German thinkers, the upcoming war was going to be a war of mobility and supply. How the hell does one train for that? Simple. Do it. The CCC did create some lovely fixtures for us to gawk at to this day. But they were the training ground of future strategists and logisticians. That was the primary mission; to learn how to organize, feed, house and move hundreds of thousands of men and their equipment for large-scale endeavors. The CCC was an experiment in wartime logistics, and a very good one.

But again, the DHS is not going to fight a foreign war. What are they training and equipping for? I'll ask again; why does the DHS have urban assault vehicles and billions of rounds of ammunition? Why is the NSA collecting EVERYONE'S communications data? What battles, er uh, contingencies are they modeling? And, *cui bono* (who benefits)? What can the governing class do with such instruments? Render itself invulnerable? To whom?

If you are going to shrink the size and reach of government and yet you allow this kind of intrusion into our personal lives and this kind of contempt for citizens, you are full of shi'ite.

16   ON WAR

Never, never, never believe any war will be smooth and easy or that anyone who embarks on that strange voyage can measure the tides and hurricanes he will encounter. The statesman who yields to war fever must realize that once the signal is given, he is no longer the master of policy but the slave of unforeseeable and uncontrollable events... incompetent or arrogant commanders, untrustworthy allies, hostile neutrals, malignant fortune, ugly surprise, awful miscalculations.
– Winston Churchill

No Jokes Here
     War is the most onerous of duties to befall a thinking and humane statesman. There may be a day when you have to come to grips with that reality. Whether you are senator voting on a war resolution or a President ordering men into

battle you will have to screw up the courage to face your duty. Or screw up the courage to stand against it, if there is the fever of violence in the land and you don't believe war to be the answer.

All the wars we have fought post-WWII have been wars of convenience, expedience or policy. We have not fought one out of necessity. Afghanistan should have been that, but we approached it like all the others.

In Korea, Vietnam, Iraq and Afghanistan the US wasted 119,174 American lives. We brought home hundreds of thousands of wounded. We killed millions of the enemy. And all for what? The tyrants we went to vanquish stayed, or the tyrants we installed betrayed us (always predictably). Borders remained as before. Countless tons of material were left behind, countless dollars squandered.

If you have the least sense of decency, the casualty numbers sicken you. If you have a brain the results should enrage you. You are witnessing the result of 70 years of post-war "yes" men; men in uniform, who ingratiated themselves to politicians with the promise of a new kind of war, limited war[51]. Clean, supposedly quick, not cheap, of course.

Robert McNamara, with his body counts and spreadsheets, promoted these guys to the head of the class and they have replicated themselves, one generation after another, ever since.

Limited War! Indeed! Great for the diplomats and officials involved. They can feel extra civilized in that they are not defeating anyone to the detriment of their self-esteem. And for the ones we kill, well they won't have a self-esteem problem, will they? It's great for the weapons industry. "Limited wars", after Korea, tend to run long and gobble up tons of product.[52] It's just one long, manageable supply chain. And "limited war" is just super for American citizens. For decades now, we've been able to hang out a flag, watch the Bob Hope USO tour and pat GI Joe on the back and call that our contribution to the effort. No draft, no rationing, no inconveniences.

Yep, it's a pretty good deal if you haven't lost a son (or now a daughter) to the "limited war". It's rather an inconvenience for the guy squatting in some shithole in Goddamistan, getting shot at, losing buddies, not seeing anything accomplished over multiple tours. And again, for the guys who get killed, well they now don't have that inconvenience anymore.

What the governing class in this country remains intentionally obtuse to is the fact that for the warriors and their families there is nothing "limited" about it at all. And when all is said and done, they know it was all for nothing.

Well, friends and neighbors, it's time we did away with "limited war". The smart candidate, when asked about the possibility of clashing with ISIS or Russia or whomever, should make one very certain point: that the President does not have the power to wage war on his own. That past Congresses have ceded power to past Presidents to have adventures in foreign lands does not make it right; not legally, not morally, not ethically. This candidate will not lift a finger against a foreign power or any agent on foreign soil until Congress specifically declares that a state of war exists between the United States and that state or entity. The only exception would the immediate defense and evacuation of Americans in a hostile area.

In a declared war, this candidate, as President, will move the might of the entire nation into the fight (and a candidate for Congress will declare support on that level). The nation will go on a war footing. The Department of Defense will be designated the Department of War. The draft will be reinstated. An overwhelming force will be marshaled. We will move on the enemy with one and only one purpose; to destroy his capability to resist our will. Victory will come in the form of a complete surrender by the enemy or his total destruction, if that is the path the enemy choses.

Pause a second to let that one sink in, look the questioner straight in the eye and say that if this is not what you expect from your commander-in-chief, you need to elect a weaker candidate. You can point out that under a weaker person, the United States is **much more likely** to be caught up in a war. And a "limited war" candidate will get more Americans killed in the course of a much longer effort. But hey, it will be a lot easier for everyone at home, especially the Congress. They can, and have in the past, turned their backs on the White House when "limited wars" became unpopular. A more uncertain President won't insist on a clean declaration of war. He'll want a reason to not fully commit.

An Approach to Actual War

Among the many things Abraham Lincoln has been lauded for, one should stand out as misguided, at least it should to a historian. That would be his "management" of war. We hear admiring stories of his going to the telegraph office every day and sitting for hours waiting for reports from the front, so worried was he, for the troops.

Well, worried he may have been, but it is clear from his communications that he was also at the telegraph office to tell his generals how they should be fighting the war. Not surprisingly, he met with one setback after another for the better part of the entire effort. All the demons mentioned in the Churchill quote at the opening of this chapter would visit the Union effort, and few understood why.

Across the divide, the confederacy was winning battles and making strides despite an economic and industrial disadvantage. While it is certain the Jeff Davis set the strategic objectives, application was correctly left to the generals. When a Southern general failed, he became more valuable to the cause, now sadder but wiser in the ways of war.

And by not being in constant communications with Davis, the troops moved rather quickly and far afield, allowing them to harass the Union one day at Winchester and a few days later, many miles away.

On the Union side, if a general failed, he was sacked. A new man took his place. Sometimes the new man was ambitious and coveted the position to begin with. Perhaps others were loyal to their old commander and took the new post with a heavy heart. It didn't matter. They still had to learn lessons they could only learn in that post. These lessons cannot be learned while observing from a subordinate position.

If I can be allowed a personal analogy, it is like conning a ship. The conning officer doesn't have his hand on the helm or the engine order telegraph. He watches the ocean, his charts, radar and other ships and gives commands to the helm. I can tell you from experience, having learned from Commander Tom Corcoran, one of the best ship handlers I've ever met, a ship feels different under your feet when you have the con than it feels when you don't. It was during a conflict in handling technique with that same man that this lesson was made most clear. He nearly relieved me in a minor emergency and would have given different orders to the helm. But he kept faith and later said that I got the exact same result as he would have gotten.

While much more complicated, commanding troops in the field has the same differences from one person to another. So the burden on the Union Army from Lincoln's telegraphs was two-fold. By replacing one general after another, there was no learning curve to rely on, and a man far-removed from the field was giving orders, to whatever general was in command at the time, on how to conduct the war. Orders were coming from a man who couldn't "feel the ship beneath his feet", so to speak.

We still have not learned our lesson on this more than 150 years later. As technology has improved, our Presidents have more and more taken over the running of warfare from the safety of the Executive Mansion, and the results have been abysmal. By crossing the lines of responsibility between strategy and tactics, policy and execution, the President becomes a burden to his troops, not a force multiplier.

So, all that said (Remember, if time allows, you should be teaching, right?) our ideal candidate will also commit to surrounding himself with the brightest, most aggressive military minds available. With their advice, the President will set the course of a war and have the generals carry out his will. This will save lives and make victory far more likely.

History agrees with me on this. For example, if Hitler wasn't delusional and had his same ambitions, he could have told his staff to take Russia and given them the supplies and support they needed. He could have fought one war at a time, as he was often cautioned to do. If he had, they'd be speaking German in Vladivostok today.

If the next Commander-in-Chief, I don't care which party he or she may be from, faces conflict or the threat of conflict with this philosophy, and doesn't take another word away from this book, I will consider my life to have been purposeful. If the same C-in-C were to face down an adversary without firing a shot, so much the better. Let's face it, when your power and resolve are undeniable, you don't have to kill anyone to protect your interests.

Oh, what a wonderful world that would be!

17 FRATRICIDE

"Thou shalt not speak ill of any Republican...Henceforth, if any Republican has a grievance against another, that grievance is not to be bared publicly. "
- California Republican Party Chairman Gaylord B. Parkinson (not Reagan).[53] This is called the 11th Commandment of the Republican Primaries.

Save Your Fire for the *Real* Opponent!

Here's the challenge we face on this subject. We are dealing with egos the size of Mount Everest. Most of the people in the race really think they should be President. Some should be satisfied with a cabinet post, a few should just go home.   For now, all are **trying** to appear Presidential.

While Democrats spew mostly untruths, they do so with real discipline. We might try to adopt some of that discipline while we speak the truth.

The choice you have when running for the nomination is to a) adopt a scorched earth policy and leave the party and everyone's bank accounts in a shambles when the primaries are over, or b) run a campaign that sets you apart from the field without pretending that everyone else in the field is the biggest POS (not an acronym for Point of Sale) since Nancy Pelosi.

Some candidates, despite pleas to the contrary and whatever attention this very chapter might gain in the wider media, will stupidly choose a). Some already have.

This is because they are not conservatives. They can barely call yourselves Republican. They don't have a solid idea or plan to call their own that will stand up to the slightest challenge.

As successful as he has been in these early days, Trump is the poster boy for that last paragraph. I have to admit that his showing a crowd Lindsay Graham's request for money and giving out Graham's phone number was pretty funny. But his lowbrow attacks against Republicans **at this stage** show him to be as odd and unserious as his haircut.

The three strongest candidates at staying on message and hitting the Democrats are Cruz, Fiorina and (sadly) Bush;[54] Fiorina, especially.

She has saved her most vociferous volleys

for Empress Rodham and the federal government in general. Her appearance on the Kelly Files showed her willingness to take on the incompetence of government head on, deal with Hillary and only argue responsibly with other GOP candidates.

Also, think about this: Let's say you (whoever you are) win the GOP nod. You've just spent the last 10 to 12 months ripping your opponents mercilessly. You know there is going to be pressure for you to take on some of these people as supporters, a veep, and as cabinet members. When you pick the one you called everything but "good guy", the public and your adversaries will know that your message was hollow. You start your first day in office, hell – your transition period - looking weak and insincere.

Finally, when all about you are yapping like skittish chihuahuas, and you rise above it and make your argument coolly, confidently but with real passion, you appear Presidential. The field appears pedantic and weak. In the early days, Bush shows a bit of promise on this point.

You must *respectfully disagree* with other Republicans; but you *abhor* the statist policies and lies of the Democrats.

The Fratricide Corollary regarding Funds and Support:

One last point: Instead of forming little cliques among conservatives running for various offices, and this goes all the way the state and local level; candidates, handlers and the Republican machine must find creative ways to show support, across the board, for conservative candidates everywhere. The party would be wise to heed this advice. There is going to be a conservative surge this year. To capitalize on it and remain relevant in coming election cycles, you will want to embrace it. Be smart, for once, instead of trying to be clever. If two known conservatives are running head-to-head, don't endorse one. Support both! A win is a win.

18 GOD-DIDDY-GOD-GOD! OMG!

"Mark my word, if and when these preachers get control of the [Republican] party, and they're sure trying to do so, it's going to be a terrible damn problem. Frankly, these people frighten me. "
- Barry Goldwater

This was originally intended to be Chapter 2, but since I know the *less broad-minded* will slam the book closed as soon as they read this, I figured I'd wait until later in the book before losing you. To the folks who think the only person worth voting for is a Christian who wears his faith on his sleeve, thanks for stopping by. But know that with the possible exception of Rick Santorum, there is no way to know if any of the candidates are what they say the are, religiously speaking.

Some political aspirants don't make a thing

of their spirituality. But too often conservatives pander to the religious right in order to "sew up the base". It's kind of the way the Dems treat blacks and Latinos. They'll go all Ebonic like Hilary and Barry do in their speeches. Or they will try to convince Hispanic citizens and legal immigrants that *illegal* immigrants are good for them because they share surnames with the illegals. Thus the Dems think they have the votes of those groups (whom they consider to be their lessers) locked up.

Note to Dems: If any of the ideas discussed here (none are new) get traction, your domination among minorities will soon end. One thing people of all races are discovering, in ever-growing numbers, is that the modern progressive is not their friend.

And thus it is slowly turning among people of faith. The Conservative = Christian crowd is shrinking. By pandering to religion for votes, you not only debase yourself and your audience, you divide the party and face the law of diminishing returns.

The prime example of this is Huck. His version of *Aw shucks, I'm just a conservative Christian* makes Reagan's affability look like Greek stoicism. This man has tarted himself up to be a conservative. He is most certainly not that.[55] He knows it, and yet he keeps the lie alive by using religion as political hackery. So what then, can be said about his *Christian* values other than the fact that they are as fungible as Bill Clinton's would be?

While the hard-core, blindly religious Billy Bobs reading this will reject it outright, the conservatives in the race ought to think twice. There are fewer and fewer Billy Bobs left in this world, even in faithful Christian families. And though he may rant on Facebook about how so-and-so isn't conservative because he doesn't go to church, Billy Bob seldom votes. His grandpa might, maybe his mother. But Billy Bobs are usually lazy, ill-informed whiners. The conservative movement burns needless energy catering to him and to abstract beliefs that don't actually underscore the secular issues we face.

Remember, our discussion on *Message*. Our target is everybody. The more narrow the target of the message, the less useful it is. Still, as I said in chapter one, be yourself. If you are a person of faith, great! Be that. But ration out the come-to-Jesus routine carefully. It wastes time and air.

I'll tell you why.

Religion is like any other exclusive group in society. In claiming membership in a group, a politician may gain some electoral traction in that specific group. But your good standing in a beach volleyball club is not going to motivate members of the Jerkwater Knitting Society.

So as a speaker, in a room full of people who kit or paly volleyball, you are left with three choices.

Pound your chest and tout how many spikes you had last year.

Do the above AND pretend to like knitting by throwing in some crap about a sweater your Aunt Helen knitted for you.

Appeal to your audience as voters and stick to the important issues.

Which would you choose? That's a silly question, because if you were a typical, modern politician, you would choose – foolishly – 1 or 2. The correct answer is 3!

WHY?

Liberals like to be pandered to. They like to be divided, subdivided and made to feel like snowflakes. They exist in a world of fallacious argument. *Republicans want ID used when voting. Democrats call Republicans racist for wanting ID. Therefore it is wrong to check the true identity of a voter.* That's the fallacy of the ad hominem argument. OR *We have to give Iran a nuke in ten years. If you disagree, what do you want WAR?* This is called a straw man argument. You can see every common fallacy in political arguments. But in the case of liberals as we have seen in recent months, they then act out on these fallacious positions. *They don't agree with us on gay marriage, abortion or the fact that races need to be pandered to. Therefor they have no right to be CEOs or to be bakers or run a pizza shop. It is okay for us to run them out of business. "They",* of course, are conservatives or Jeffersonian liberals.

This also demonstrates solipsism on the part of liberals. When they look in the mirror, they think they are looking at the world. If you deviate, you are evil.

Earlier, I said that by teaching people to be republican (members of American society) you can produce Republicans (members of a party). Here is where you can do the most good. By delivering a full-throated, muscular message, honestly and clearly, a lot of the liberals I mention above will have a positive alternative to emotionalism and anger. Where do you think those folks known as the neo-cons came from?

Clear-minded conservatives and uncommitted voters do not think like progressives. We have real jobs. We are concerned with real issues. We want to know what the hell you intend to do in office. We don't like the baby kissing and the *I'm-a-shuffle-board-enthusiast-like-you* routine. We tolerate it. We wait to get past the pandering garbage to hear what you have to say about the economy, the size of government, America's enemy's and/or Bill Clinton's former 1970s sex partner, Hillary. We don't want hugs and drum circles. We want your thoughts and plans on real shit!

For the record, no one likes shuffleboard. Even people who play it everyday hate it. They only do it because they have no athletic skills. I'm great at it.

Somebody Wake Up That Guy in the Back.

I want the handlers as well as the candidates to pay attention here. It goes against common assumptions and requires a shift in thinking to get used to.

As illustrated above, people don't really care about your religious views if you are not from the identical religion. Let me say that again for the folks in the back. PEOPLE DON'T REALLY CARE ABOUT YOUR RELIGIOUS VIEWS IF YOU ARE NOT FROM THE IDENTICAL RELIGION.

It only becomes a topic of discussion because it is considered polite, God only knows why(pun fully intended), when someone says something spiritual, to compliment them on it. The substance is unimportant and the compliment is as well-intentioned as a reflexive, "God bless you," when someone sneezes. But it will not get you enough votes to win national office.

There is an even less desirable way a candidate's religious pandering can inspire conversation. If the larger public senses animus or religious provincialism, no matter how minor or benign, those people will be turned off by the candidate. And they might say so. I would contend that if honest, **most** people would say they wouldn't vote for a guy if they perceive him as **too** religious. The few that make up the radical wing of the religious right would. *Many folks would not vote for a candidate who is overly solicitous of a religious audience.* Candidates are better served educating voters on the folly of identity politics.

I like Ted Cruz. He is almost always the smoothest, smartest duck in the room. He appears to be a man of substance, his Catholic priest delivery not withstanding. Contrary to popular lore, he has held an executive position. As Solicitor General he had to absorb and digest information all day long. After doing so, he made decisions and delegated authority to see them carried out. This is much better preparation for the White House than being an absentee legislator or sitting with buddies in Chicago writing bogus grants for each other to cash in on worthless government programs; the Barry Obama resume. I am of a mind that Cruz would be a very good VP choice.

Still, it is arguable that Ted Cruz did serious damage to his candidacy by announcing at Liberty University. There is just so much wrong here. By speaking to the audience as "us", and putting *strong* religious overtones in his announcement speech, he implies that he favors this group over any other. My assessment will put off many Christian talking heads, but the reader knows it is true. You cannot be parochial and all-welcoming at the same time. No matter how many phrases you insert about *people of all faiths*, it still smacks of *vote for me and I'll give you the best darn Christian theocracy ever! And...oh, yeah...we still like Jews and Muslims and Druids and Atheists and other Christian denominations too...even Catholics.*

The point is that making more than a mere passing mention of your faith, and in direct context with something important about you, and only you, you are wasting time and energy in a way that could easily blow up in your face.

Never announce your candidacy or break open a new stump speech at a church or mosque or temple or universities dedicated to associate faiths. Do it at the Washington Monument (everyone's monument) or the Statue of Liberty (everyone's statue) or before an Eagles' game (everyone's team[56]).

Finally, this kind of phony intimacy feeds the undesirable narrative that as President; you would be involved directly in the lives of everyday people, or at least their pal in DC. This is exactly the wrong message to send to the listener. It is also a form of identity politics...always horseshit. Always. Leave the preaching and the halleluiahs to the preacher and the choir. You are seeking a secular office for **all the people**. You're not running for Pope.

To the voters:

It sounds cynical to say this, but politicians love a religious constituency. And it's not out of the purity of their hearts. The more people there are that believe the zanier aspects of all religions, the more a politician knows your credulity can be counted on. You might actually believe **they are** "with the government and here to help. "

The typical political hacks are the type I describe at the beginning of the chapter. They will whore themselves out to anyone on any subject so they can join the governing class and set themselves up for life.

The honest ones, precious few, know that they can't deal with your personal religious foibles. When they get to DC they find their plate is full just dealing with real-world problems, and a lot more than praying will have to be done about them. If you have such a representative you may want to dump him because he doesn't pander to "God" enough. You do so at your own peril. The next hack is watching and will be happy to swoop in wrapped in a flag and carrying a cross. He won't do for you what the religiously unidentifiable guy will do. The hack will take your vote and forget you exist.

To come to terms with this reality, we need to acknowledge what the modern political animal is. To survive more than a few states during primary season, a candidate must be of a coldly calculating mind and have a gargantuan ego. There might be something out there more important than they are, but they (the politicians) are near, if not at, the center of the universe. Those who lack this *"quality"* don't often survive. So a REAL spiritual candidate is a much rarer species than one might think.

So whether you are religious or not, the next

time a politician tells you he is motivated by Jesus, Yahweh, Allah or a talking tree, ask him what he plans to do about the deficit? Surely his spirit guides have addressed at least that issue while calling him to serve, eh?

Don't let your faith be fodder for insult and manipulation by disingenuous hacks. Hold them to account no matter whom they claim to worship!

19 ON REACHING ACROSS THE AISLE

"Let me just say this. The Republican Party is being told to be the party of no. No more stimulus spending. No cap-and-trade. No card check. None of this other stuff. Gridlock is not an American problem. It's an American achievement. The framers of our Constitution didn't want an efficient government; they wanted a safe government. To which end they filled it with slowing and blocking mechanisms. Three branches of government, two branches of the legislative branch, veto, veto override, supermajority, judicial review.... What I'm saying...is that when we have gridlock, the system is working".
– George Will

"Go fuck yourself"[57]
 – Dick Cheney to Patrick Leahy on the Senate

floor.

One of the multitudinous false narratives that seem to grip the American psyche is the mean-spirited Republican Party. For the Democrats, this is one of the great Orwellian achievements of the last 60 years. With a talent for taking the truth and turning it 180 degrees (no President has supported Israel more than I have...we are stronger and more respected than any time in history...vast right-wing conspiracy...most transparent administration in history...) Democrats have made a science of vitriolic, completely fabricated attacks on Republicans. When the right counters the phony attack, let's say on Obama, the left says, "See what haters they are? How dare you disagree with Dear Leader (Obama, not Kim)! They only do that because they are racists!"

"Racist" is their favorite charge among the many. In the past few weeks, Bill's homely wife has been skulking around the country saying that the Republican Party is actively denying minorities the opportunity to vote. Only the most ignorant members of the left wing base believe this. There is not a single program, of either party and certainly not of the Republicans, that impedes anyone's ability to vote. Not a single one. There are bills the right wing wants passed that will prevent Hilary's operatives from arranging for people to vote illegally. So what does a party do when they want to rig an election and the opposing party says they shouldn't? Scream "racism," of course.

This is addressed to candidates running for Congress and their voters. Extending your hand to people like this, who are beneath your dignity, is a waste of time. Jim Webb? Sure. Harry Reid? No way.

In an effort to portray themselves as people the media will like, Republicans, especially weak ones, talk about how they can work with the other side to get things done. McCain made a career of it and called it being a "maverick". He said it would serve him well in his presidential bid because people on both side of the aisle loved him, and the press knew he was a good guy. That lasted until his nomination started to gel. From that day until the end of the election, the attacks from the political left, including their simple servants in the media, never let up.

So I would caution you against promising to work across the aisle in an effort to seduce the press. You will look stupid later when you say you are for school vouchers for minorities and the press and the entire democratic party call you a racist and a hater because you want to pull little black children out of the hell-hole schools the Democrats insist they stay in. For now, it is best to avoid the subject of close cooperation altogether. If asked, say (truthfully) that there will be specific times where you may be able to work with certain Democrats to move important legislation, but the Democrats will have to earn your trust first.

Don't be afraid to say that they haven't done a good job of it lately. But be ready to meet the opposition halfway on that rare occasion when they have a constructive idea.

Shutdowns

Two of my favorite commentators are George Will and Charles Krauthammer. When given an opportunity to address an issue, they usually knock it out of the park. And they make it look so easy.

So you can imagine my dismay at seeing them get it wrong, time after time, on the issue of government shutdowns.

For the record, the last shutdown shouldn't really count because everyone got paid in full. All of the "non-excepted" workers, which is to say, mostly unnecessary federal employees, got their full back pay. They got an unscheduled, paid vacation and it didn't cost them an hour's worth of vacation time. And nobody missed them.

In the lead-up to the pretend shutdown, it was clear to everyone that it was Obama who was being intransigent and petulant. During that time, the Republicans approached the White House[58] repeatedly with compromises. Obama simply ran out the clock by refusing to budge on a single one. He has never compromised on a meaningful level with Republicans. The Republican half of the four morons showed just how feckless and weak they are as leaders during these days.

But it shouldn't have mattered. We have had two shutdowns and one episode where the imperial President and the Dem lackeys in Congress passed major legislation in ways devoid of ethics and without the cooperation of the "means-spirited" Republicans. These were all followed by landslide victories for...that's right, Republicans.

And yet, with the Democrats clearly creating and sustaining this standoff, Will and Krauthammer joined the chorus of cowards begging the Republicans to not force a shutdown. WTF? Do these guys not recall previous standoffs and showdowns with arrogant, under-qualified

Presidents?

To the candidate, Congressional or Presidential: With the least provocation (or if possible raise the issue yourself) say that in the event the Democrats try, to once again, thwart the budget process, you will not only go to the mattresses on the issue, you will personally lock some of the doors and send the workers home yourself. You will point out the chicanery and dishonesty that got the government to such a point. There will be no back pay for returning workers. Their light paychecks will be the work of the Democrats. No departments will be "plussed up" to make up any hardships suffered by a shutdown on your watch. When the Dems are acting like petulant Occupy Sissy Street children, don't stop them. Hold them up to ridicule.

As before when discussing *Other People's Money* and *Message*, the American people understand this kind of honesty and toughness. Your reward will be a landslide in the following election.

Let me remind you, this book is not about the 2016 election. It is about using this election and your work after it to set up years, perhaps decades of success.

Gridlock

More to what is my natural tendency, I agree with everything Will said at the opening of this chapter. To go him one better:

Given the sewage that Congress has smeared all over the Federal Code in the last two decades...

Given the theatrical acrimony over everything that passes through both houses...

Given the wretched *things* that have been placed in cabinet positions, the federal bench and the UN in recent years...

...I say **gridlock is king!**

Until we have honest brokers in leadership of both parties in Congress and until we have a President who respects the legislative process, we are far better off with these 535 people naming post offices or just sitting on their hands altogether.

A President is not the 536th legislator. He has a job to do carrying out the laws that already exist. And no one begrudges his possible desire to suggest legislation. But he is not needed on Capitol Hill until they have a bill for him to sign. That distance should be respected. The country would be infinitely better off for it.

Do you know there was a time when senators were appointed by their respective states? They were not popularly elected. The very thought of it...sniff, sniff, sigh.

20 WRAP-UP

Liberals have created, and the minority leadership has exploited, a community of dependent people, unaware of the true route to prosperity and happiness: self-reliance and self-investment. Instead, people are told that America is unjust, unfair, and full of disadvantages. They are told that their only hope is for government to fix their problems. What has happened is that generations of people have bought into this nonsense and as a result have remained hopelessly mired in poverty and despair -- because the promised solutions don't work. And they will never work -- they never have. - Rush Limbaugh

One of the overriding points of Liberal Fascism is that all of the totalitarian "isms" of the left commit the fallacy of the category error. They all want the state to be something it cannot be. They passionately believe the government can love you, that the state can be your God or your church or your tribe or your parent or your village or all of these things at once. Conservatives occasionally make this mistake, libertarians never do, liberals almost always do. -- Jonah Goldberg[59]

30 July 2015

In the last few weeks, Trump, Pataki, Kasich and Jindal have announced.

Trump leads in the polls.

The Intel IG found **classified** information in messages from Clinton's personal, **unclassified** (and illegal) server.

Obama has gone to the UN to get his treaty, that isn't a treaty, with Iran blessed and is ignoring his own legislature. And you thought my comments about his loyalties were over the top, didn't you?

Rand Paul has a flat tax plan out.

Cruz called McConnell (one of the four morons) a liar.

In a dust up with Walker on the Iran deal, Bush appears to be the appeaser. Sad.

HRC's campaign announced that the Republican they really fear as an opponent is Kasich. Since a day doesn't pass without Hilarity making a central point that isn't one hundred and eighty degrees out from the truth, what does that tell you about Kasich? They know can beat him.

For the Iran Nuke deal, Huckabee accused Obama of walking the Jews back to the ovens with his dismissal of Israel and collusion with the Iranians against the interests of the United States. When challenged, he doubled down. Good job, Huck. I am not a supporter but you are being the distraction. And you bloody well got Geraldo Rivera's goat. He practically went to blows on *The Five* with Eric Bolling over the issue.

10 August 2016

A lot has happened in the last year. We are down to four viable candidates for president. The down-ticket for conservatives is looking wobbly thanks to the presence of Trump. Hillary has successfully used the FBI and the "Justice" Department to protect her from what should have been a slam-dunk prosecution over her illegal server. It remains to be seen what might become of the Clinton's whoring the office of Secretary of State for her "foundation", but if past is prologue, she'll continue on her merry way.

Two candidates have validated the main message of the original edition of this book. Sadly, one of them only embodied the first two chapters. Trump certainly didn't shy away from controversy. He used it to stand out from the crowd. He didn't sugar coat his message. But his use of my ideas ends before chapter 3. More on him in a bit.

Bernie Sanders, as stated in the forward of this book, made his candidacy a case study of ALL of the points in this book. He remained himself throughout the campaign. Except for the fatal, early dismissal of Clinton's emails, he didn't worry about making waves. He stated his case as he saw it. He explained his points. He even did a little teaching along the way. None of it was correct and his Socialist ideas mark him as a statist failure. Still, he managed to create a large and loyal following.

The Rhetorical Power Curve

It is time we reestablished the language of real political discourse on our own terms. For decades now, we have given credibility to the empty rhetoric of the left and in contending with them, used terms, phrases and arguments that make no sense on their face, so fall flat even faster when trying to combat the leftist terms. Welfare and separate treatment equaling empowerment, vacillation and appeasement equaling negotiation, strength equaling warmongering, success equaling greed. Then there's everyone's favorite: abortion equals women's health (I guess the only time a woman is unhealthy is when she is pregnant). To employ these and a thousand other such phrases into our argument, to say we're a better version of these things, requires an apologist's approach to a contest.

Get back to conservative basics. Use real terms for things you are for and against; free market, military power vs. the welfare state, weakness. Don't say the U. N. can be a tool for good and that you hope to work with it to blah, blah, blah. . . Say it is a joke in its present state and you'll see it fixed or see it gone.

Don't promise a law or a policy to satisfy every human desire. Tell people, directly, to stand on their own two feet and do for themselves. Don't look for opportunities for the government to do more. Announce your plan to see a government that does very little, because the people are so strong and independent that they resent the intrusion. Express admiration for those in this country who see things that way. And, YES, at the possible expense of the feelings of those who don't. Don't offer excuses for those who don't participate as full members of the society. Don't tell them that race or past circumstances or living in a poor town dictates their future. Tell them that they are the arbiters of their fortune. Challenge Americans to be strong. Dare them to become something.

I've heard it said that if you give a man a reputation he will live up to it. So do it. Speak of the New American. Talk about men and women from every corner of society that are educating themselves, working and excited about the future! Let people know, especially young people, that in the game of life this is a really cool club to belong to. Praise the trades and professions equally. Don't be timid about it.

Jobs

When discussing budget cuts, tax cuts, regulation and compliance, I repeatedly spoke of the jobs we will create with these changes to our laws. I would like to think most people understand this implicitly. But I will expound a bit, just to be thorough.

First, we won't really be *creating* the jobs. No government can create a single, real, market-economy job. Government can create make-work, tax-draining jobs until the cows come home. But only entrepreneurs can create real jobs.

It is the mission of all true conservatives to

stay completely out of the way of honest job creators. And all the ideas discussed here are intended to facilitate just that.

If you slash the cost of tax compliance across the board, you leave billions of dollars in the hands of people who have the talent and motivation to hire workers. It is the same with regulatory compliance.

When you invite overseas cash home to a welcoming environment, you create an economy where there is as much money, or more, as there are people to earn it. When you take a meat cleaver to the government programs and departments that don't work, and cut taxes accordingly, you leave money in the hands of people that can make the money work as it should.

None of this is a "maybe". These are hard and fast economic realities. They are as certain as gravity. With all their equating business and hard work with greed, the left has been trying to stifle the free market and gather more power through government dependency. They craft their message in an attempt deny these basic economic realities. It is shocking how many people don't understand the most fundamental concepts of the free market. Teach. Teach. Teach.

Make it your own.

This book was written for the politician as well as the voter. The idea was to suggest ways to liven the debate, encourage candidates to be themselves and seek victory by taking on the important issues in an honest fashion. It is also my hope that the candidates will take my admonishments about teaching to heart. I think we can say we've had a few laughs along the way.

Let me reiterate, this is by no means a complete list of what candidates can do to become successful. But it is a very good start. And it is in the general "mechanics" of what I've tried to convey that you can not only win, but win with coattails. Be yourself. Be audacious. Lean in. Touch noses. Be the distraction.

Why do you think "the Donald" spent the first several weeks of his campaign at the top of the polls? Is it his eloquence? Is it his quiet, intellectual tone? Is it that he is too shy to make a splash? Seriously.

He was, and at the time of this writing, is filling a void. I told you that the American voters are aching for a politician to come along and INSPIRE them, be HONEST with them and not blow sunshine up their asses.

Everyone knows in his or her heart of hearts

that Trump is a great real estate investor with a penchant for circus. But they also know he's the kind of guy who will get into a public, middle school catfight with a huge New York landmark like Rosie O'Donnell. What real guy would do that? It was embarrassing to watch. Still I will state for the record, I would vote for Trump over HRC without batting an eyelid.

Trump is striking a nerve because he is the distraction. He can be unseated and any candidate can ride from here to victory just by taking on the real federal issues (budget, taxes, the economy, national security, smaller government) as loudly as Trump. Where he employs brash braggadocio, you employ humor, facts and strong delivery. Kick your speechwriters in the ass and tell them you want some soaring Churchillian prose to go with the key issues, and some brash humor.

Trump knows marketing. Market yourself with his passion and add your own class and style.

And for goodness sake, focus your fire on the political left!

Trump, as an Example of Voter Vetting

I am going to ask some questions about the Trump candidacy. Make no mistake; I am not

STREET POLITICS: It Ain't Your Daddy's GOP Anymore!

like the crew of the Blaze saying they will never vote for Trump. If Trump wins the Republican nomination, you may find me out there pounding the pavement for him.

And I would encourage you to be as tough on all the candidates as I am being on "the Donald" right now. You need to be coldly calculating. You are not leafing through wallpaper swatches here. Take a long look at the one-trick ponies in the race. You may REALLY like them, but to build a better America, you may have to jettison them in favor of a candidate who can work on a wider array of issues to create a government half its present size, which I would consider a good start.

That said, it is time for me to be a wet rag. There is a great deal about Trump which has not been thoroughly established yet, primary among which are the concerns expressed in the following three questions:

Is he serious or is he just polishing his brand?

Is he the type of rich egomaniac who is just positioning for a third party run?

Is he a shill for Calamity Clinton and positioning for the third party run a foregone conclusion?

(Questions 2 or 3 above, answered in the

affirmative, will have the same result; Bill Clinton as First Lady.)

To date, Trump's politics, contributions and attitude don't provide the answers. So I would caution the voter about getting too caught up in the hype before we see some real policy positions and concrete plans fleshed out. For the record, I hope I am completely out to lunch on this one. It would be great to see that Trump was in it for the long haul.

10 August 2016

We no longer need to worry about a third party run by Trump. But we still have Trump. As predicted here and at streepolitics.us, the media is now hitting its stride in covering the Trump campaign. A Trump vs. Clinton general election was exactly the scenario they dreamt about since last June. The media carried the Donald for the entire year. They were happy to take him to task on blatantly liberal issues. They knew that by attacking him on taxes or immigration they would make him more popular with part of the right wing; the part that doesn't really understand conservatism, but they drool like Pavlov's dogs when they hear the word "conservative". It was very clear to anyone paying attention a year ago that Trumps inability to express a clear thought and his thin skin would work to cause friction in the Republican Party. Over the ensuing year, he has shown he was even more shallow, petulant and willing to hack up fellow Republicans than even I gave him credit for.

There were four or five occasions during the primary on which we were assured that the girlie tantrums and tweets were behind us and that we would see a more presidential Trump. Except for four or five teleprompter speeches, we saw nothing of the sort.

These attributes make my point about the press carrying Trump self-evident. He was every bit the Reality TV clown in June of '15 that he is today. The press knew pretty much everything about Trump as they do today. They say he's crazy now; unstable and erratic. He was all of that 14 months ago. There are still reports to come late this summer about his mob ties. The press has been sitting on that for years. Was it the case with any other candidate where the press would split screen an empty podium for half an hour, twice (or more) a week, waiting for a campaign event? No, of course not. But they did it for Trump. The media turned a seventeen-person primary into wall-to-wall Trump. The intent was to have a candidate they could eviscerate in the fall. And that's what they are going to do.

Let's revisit the comments made last year, and many times since, about Trump the shill. At no point has Trump said anything to allay the suspicion. I'm not saying *I know* he was a willing fly in the ointment to support the Democrats and corrupt politicians like McConnell. But if we saw video tomorrow of his campaign huddling with Zeke Emanuel and Bill Clinton, the objective observer would not be the least bit shocked. The Republican ticket spends 5 days a week trying to clean up the mess made the day before. This is either shocking incompetence or the work of a dogged shill. Is Trump in a fixed fight? Did he agree to put on a good show, throw some hard punches at the opponent, but not make enough adult sense to give the Republicans the White House? Or is he just mind-blowingly inept? I would defy anyone to demonstrate where Trump has consistently made sense and didn't hurt the party brand for more than 48 hours in the last 14 months. He hasn't. There is no third possibility.

And how did we get this far into a campaign with such an egregiously incapable candidate to represent us on the right? The answer is found in the opening pages of this book. I have said many times here and elsewhere, well before this election, the American people were completely fed up with formulaic, well-handled, risk-averse candidates. It is a coincidence - happy or not, depending on your point of view – that they reached the limit of their tolerance now. They were thirsty for a brash, in-your-face campaign where the hero was not afraid the throw the bullshit flag on the entire system. They were longing for that man or woman. In the absence of an articulate adult with those qualities, they ran to Trump. His name-calling and mindless tweets were seen as "telling it like it is."

Most people, even Trump supporters, know the Donald doesn't really know what "it is" to begin with. His campaign, his supporters on TV and radio, and his loyal fans spend every conversation about the man trying to explain what Trump *meant* to say yesterday. Almost without fail, their explanation is a totally new concept, often well thought out, but *completely disconnected* from the tangential rant they are trying to explain on Trump's behalf.

Trump carried the primaries and will likely loose the White House to a felon with no genuine sense of other, because the other seventeen candidates designed their campaigns around an idea that the voters now consider an insult. If Rand Paul had come out of the gates swinging; if he were just as loud as Trump, while employing his own sharp mind and well-developed ideas **against democrats and Trump**, we would have had a different race. If Carly Fiorina had used Trump's attack style **against Democrats and Trump,** and her own real world experience, and got in the news every day, we'd have three women running for president today? If the entire primary field, instead of trying to be the Neville Chamberlains of American politics, called Trump for the cartoonish child that he is the day he announced, we'd have somebody running as the Republican nominee. But it wouldn't be Donald Trump.

And yes, Rubio and Cruz did take their shots late in the game, but by then it looked forced. They had spent too much energy trying not to lock horns with Trump. What none of them understood was when Trump attacked someone, his numbers went up; but so did the numbers for the target of the attack. When they fought back as Carly did once, their numbers would climb as much as Trump's. But there, in the background, were the formulaic handlers. *Don't make him mad, be his friend, don't mix it up with him,* the handlers would tell the candidates. Result? A liberal with slightly fewer tax brackets than Clinton's tax plan heads the Republican ticket.

Single Issue Voting = 0

One of the weakest links in any election is the single-issue voter. These are the most shortsighted of any voter. While I'm glad they vote, I will caution them on any single-issue position as I did people who vote for a guy because they think he is religious. It is too easy for a political hack to poll an issue and say that he's the guy for that issue. For one thing, the same candidate will probably have to back peddle and say that he is something else in another venue while pandering to *those* people. Rodham/Clinton does it and doesn't even know she's supposed to be embarrassed.

While naval gazing and playing with your single issue, you may miss the candidate with greater ability on a wider range of issues that will let you live your life as you see fit.

I'm only going to vote for a guy who promises to end abortion[60].

Well great. So you send a candidate to DC with an extremely narrow mandate and no political will or cache to pursue all the other things that are holding this country back. Is that the drill? Well, say hello to permanent Obamacare and government-funded abortions for as far as the eye can see. Say hello to failing schools, the four morons and Hilary for President until the next time conservatives have this opportunity to change the system. Good job!

May I suggest we use the Buckley formula: Find the most ***<u>electable conservative</u>*** in the primary and vote for him. Did you see what I did with those two words? Highlighted, bolded and underlined. That's a hint. Huckabee is a one or two trick pony. Those tricks are popular among the conservative base. But guys like him won't be President. By all means, keep your argument alive for the issues you care about, but the object here is to create a government *more conservative and effective* than the present government. We'll fight the remaining battles once we're in power (with a veto proof majority).

10 August 2016

Well the one we picked is neither a conservative, nor is he at this point, electable. He has 90 days to grow up and fly right (pun intended). We'll see.

Voters! Here's an idea. VOTE!

In my previous job, as you may well imagine, I was the guy who always had an opinion about politics. I can safely say the overwhelming majority of my fellow employees were right or center-right, politically. We often had discussions where we would agree with each other vehemently and loudly. You can imagine what they are like.

But I can also say the vast majority of those folks didn't vote. The biggest reason I hear from people who don't vote, especially conservatives, is that it doesn't make a difference. "They're all the same. " I hear that one a lot. Think, damn it! We're paying top dollar for our government. It's like saying, "I'll pay you the $200 but I won't bother to pick my fantasy football team, they're all the same anyway."

There are two things wrong with that position. The first is they are not ALL the same. Most Americans will now agree, with some real regret that a Romney presidency would have been far better than four more years with Barry. We all knew that to be so, and yet so many people failed to vote. Yes, I said failed. I'm not the sweet type who will say, "well gee, if that's the way you feel"... Hey! The folks that stayed home knew the score. In not voting they failed themselves and their country. To be sure, they failed their city, county and state in those elections as well.

The other problem with the previously stated position is those who don't vote may want to see a certain candidate win or see changes made, but they are just too damn lazy to get up and do something as simple as cast a damn ballot.

Say what you want about all the people in politics. At every level and in all parties, individuals get out there and get pounded by the media, conservatives especially. But they all have to take the pounding when people speak poorly of them. I know I've thrown some zingers at them here and don't apologize for a single one. But in our circus of an election cycle, these people beat their brains out for years to try and advance an agenda.

Don't be that guy. Don't be the citizen who stays home out of laziness and tries to sound cool by acting cynical. "Dude, they're all the same. " Get the hell out there and vote! It's just one day. They even have early voting.[61] It's an important franchise. It costs lots of your tax dollars to maintain and execute every two years. Worst case, you can say you at least took a stand. Win or loose, you weren't sitting on your hands like a spoiled, petulant brat, wanting something and not doing your part to get it.

In all fairness I will say the Four Morons may make an aware citizen rather cynical about politics. The Morons are corrupt and devoid of scruples. But the answer to that isn't skipping the vote. By voting in huge numbers we embolden the class we send to DC. With a strong mandate it will be as easy as breathing to dump Reid, Pelosi, McConnell and Boehner (now Ryan).

It's Not Just About the White House!

This year, more than any since FDR, voting a conservative down-ticket is critical to pulling the country back onto its feet. That admonition goes out to moderate (read Not Socialist) Democrats as well. If we let the felon get into the Oval Office with Reid and Pelosi running the legislature, even thinking Democrats know the result will be corruption across the board and the rape of the treasury. JFK liberals know as well as Regan conservatives that at some point, we must draw a line and turn back toward responsibility. But we crossed that line years ago. We must send disciplined, fiscal conservatives to DC this year. If we don't we won't recognize our country four years from now. Chuckle at that last sentence if you want to, but where have I missed a prediction in this book? Where have I misread the mood of the country? Have I been wrong in my assessments, even if you disagree with my suggested solutions? I haven't. So keep reading.

As for the Republicans, we will likely not get

the White House this year. Unless Hillary has a complete meltdown, or someone in government gets guts and a sense of duty and has her arrested, Trump will be a carcass rotting in the desert by late October.

But as you consider what's been said here, ask yourself if we've learned anything. Has the political class learned anything? If this year has come and gone with nothing to show for it, there is only one person in your life you can blame. That would be you.

By involving ourselves in the public square we stand the only chance of being the voice that can carry these lessons into towns, counties and maybe to the White House. By remaining silent or sitting in our Facebook echo chambers, we simply guarantee the continued disintegration of good governance and effective politics. I'll repeat: This book is a primer intended to inspire action well into the future. Regardless of what comes in November, the future is still ours to make, *if we want to!*

A Final Note on Lithuanians

I don't know many Lithuanians. Do you? It's not like everyone puts on "kiss me, I'm Lithuanian" buttons and gets hammered at the pub on St. Casimir Day. The few Lithuanians I do know are very sweet people, seriously. But I've never heard a Lithuanian joke. Not one. So I figure it was their turn in the barrel. And I made up the story about the antique shop.

I was thinking about picking on Croatians in my next book. But I have a Croatian nephew. He's a big guy. He could probably drive my narrow, white ass into the ground like a tent peg. Anyway, you can bet I'll be breaking somebody's stones.

Make It last.

As I scribble, I have a contractor restoring an old workshop behind my house. I flatter myself to say I build furniture. As a side business, I made a zingin' $2000 over five or six years.

I hope the writing pays off. Did I say that out loud?

The building is a 50 year-old pole barn. The bones are in good shape but there was some rot in key areas that had to be fixed before installing the new roof and siding. My contractor[62] was tickled at the idea of saving the old building. I couldn't have built one as nice as this one was in its glory days. Before starting the job, he told me he could give me a 25-year roof but couldn't promise a 25-year building. If I want the building to be here when I'm an old man, I have to take care of it.

I am basically telling the reader the same thing. We (politicians and voters) have seen conservative passions flare and die several times over the last few decades. What happened to the mom-and-pop wing of the Tea Party movement? Where was everyone in 2012? If we use what we learn here, we can win. But if we don't do the heavy lifting consistently, if we don't keep our message fresh and relevant, if we lose the passion and revert to business-as-usual after the big win, our party will roll to a stop before 2018. The voters will feel burned, and rightfully so. If we don't hit DC ready to "get them by the balls and kick them in the ass", we and our victory will go down as another hollow chapter in American political history at a time when so much needed to be done.

ABOUT THE AUTHOR

A native of Yeadon, Pennsylvania, Matt Jordan has spent his adult years in service to the United States. That included 23 years in the U.S. Navy and 14 years as a contract employee for the Department of Defense. He has seen service in Southern Europe, North Africa, and the Middle East.
The author has retired with his wife, Lynette to Vancleave, Mississippi where he spends his time writing and building furniture. This is an updated release of his first book.

The Author is host of *Streetpolitics.us* and a travel writer for *hubpages.com/@mattjordan iii*

END NOTES

Ch. 1

[1] *Blacklisted: The Untold Story of Joe McCarthy and his Fight Against America's Enemies*, M. Staunton Even, Random House, 2007

[2] *Treason: Liberal Treachery from the Cold War to the War on Terrorism,* Ann Coulter, Three Rivers Press, 2003

Ch. 2

[3] Announced 24 June

[4] Announced 30 June

[5] *Minimum Wage Laws = Minimum Thinking,* Matthew Jordan, *Pedestrian Politics and Economics,* 3 March 2014

[6] I often wonder if they put heroine in Wawa coffee. Neither I, nor my extended family, nor most of the people I grew up with, can pass a Wawa without *jonesing* for a 16 ouncer.

[7] I am only going to say this once. I was raised

on the grammatically convenient masculine when talking about persons generally. I am not going to sprinkle sugar on your ass by ham-handedly inserting "his or her" or "he and she" with every nameless, genderless example I provide. It's patronizing and reads like shit. Do not kid yourself into thinking I don't care about Fiorina or Bill Clinton's old lady.

[8] In 2010, Barbara Boxer interrupted a general testifying before her committee. He had used the term "Ma'am" while answering a question. It is quite common to use official titles intermingled with sir or ma'am in testimony so as not to be saying senator, senator, senator for hours on end. But Old Babbs was having none of that! She had just watched a rerun of *A Few Good Men* and was dying for a chance to make someone feel like her lesser while in her august presence. It's just one example of DC egos run amuck: and a funny one. Check it on YouTube.

[9] Pelosi, Reid, Boehner and McConnell

Ch. 3

[10] In this book, I am referring to the liberal doctrinaire who populates the left-wing governing class. I have liberal friends who I love and respect. But they are not members of the political elite in the mold of Clinton (female half), Obama (either half).

---

[11] I will reject out-of-hand the typical qualifiers I usually hear at this point. Comments like, well he just got lucky, or what if he just inherited everything. Luck is how the jealous describe the success of others. And if the richest guy in town inherited what he has, find out what his parents or grandparents did. Such wealth rarely lasts three generations.

[12] For the record, I don't own a Nazi flag and I am glad the country was reunited after the civil war. And, well, my sister is really hot.

[13] Can you guess which disgusting, two-faced, lard ass I am referring to?

[14] I read the Drudge report. It is one of my favorite websites and is an excellent source of information. But my self-confidence as a conservative comes from bouncing my arguments off of sites which do not agree with me. It is how I expand my knowledge base and check for possibilities that may exist outside my own thinking.

Ch. 4

[15] What do they have on Roberts? Do they have video of him snorting coke, playing with hookers or taking bribes? Or his he just trying to be co-President and get his name written in bold print

in the history books? Either way, he is a disgrace to the court. See *Obama's Top 50 What?!* At my blog, *Pedestrian Politics and Economics*

[16] Don't laugh. There has been such legislation debated. The federal website www. stopbullying.gov says "The U. S. Department of Education's Office for Civil Rights has released several guidance letters on the obligation for schools to address harassment and specific considerations for sexual harassment, disability harassment, and denial of FAPE. " So even without insane legislation regulating children on the playground and big, fat meanies on the Internet, the government is threatening schools, states and counties with keeping more of their money over this bullshit issue.

[17] There is no point where "gay" puts you among or disqualifies you from being a conservative. So let's not box out yet another group from our numbers.

Ch. 5

[18] Example Aetna and Obama care. They sat down often with Jonathan Gruber, et al and designed a law making Aetna one of the agents of the government, operating the new government medical insurance industry known as Obamacare.

[19] In the first release of this book, I favored a flat tax and no automatic withholding. You would pay your tax at the end of the year. This was one of those ideas that works great until you add people to the mix. As my friend Joe, a financial advisor points out, many people would simply spend their money, having nothing left at tax time. Because so many Americans have been conditioned to be consumers without consequence, we'd quickly become Greece. Even quicker than we will on the present system.

[20] This acronym shouldn't be confused with another common usage as in, "Boy, that Sharpton! What a POS!"

[21] According to the Census Bureau table 475, **Federal Government Receipts by Source**, as of 2011 total receipts were $2. 174 trillion. While the retail market has grown since then, it probably hasn't grown as much as our big federal piggy. With retail sales in the neighborhood of $5 trillion per year, replacing government receipts would require an enormous.

Ch. 6

[22] More on this when we discuss ending party fratricide.

[23] If W were brighter than a 40-watt bulb, he'd

have understood that true conservatism is already the most compassionate (or put more correctly – benevolent) system of governing. We didn't need yet another bullshit education program. We needed to get the federal government out of the education business completely. It has never educated a single child. And the more money we throw at the problem, the worse it has gotten. If Bush, 41 and 43, had done nothing more than spend their time fighting to slash the size of the federal code, we'd have been far better off than we are today. This, despite the 2008 bank scam and eight years of Wall Street's favorite son, Barry Obama.

[24] This is an irresponsible process with which I disagree. Further, sequestration was not a cut in spending on anything. It was a reduction on the anticipated increase. This is automatic and a product of another irresponsible process called baseline budgeting. That's been around for decades. No person calling himself a conservative should EVER vote for anything that starts with automatic spending increases across the board before budget deliberations even begin.

Ch. 7

[25] The point being that he could have simply kept the army and taken over as dictator. You can be sure there were more then a few who worried

over such a possibility.

[26] Again, that would be Boehner, McConnell, Pelosi and Reid

[27] This abbreviation is common and serves to distinguish it from the Department of Energy (DOE). The similarity to a dysfunction afflicting half of middle-aged men is just a funny coincidence.

[28] According to *Shutdown lowdown: Sizing up the federal furloughs* by Yuval Rosenberg, The Fiscal Times 7 Oct 2013, As many as 800,000 workers were initially affected by the last government shutdown. The Pentagon called some of them back to work early. Did you miss any of them? An event known as Snowmageddon 2010 shut down the federal government for a week. It was that week, the governing class noticed a PR mistake when refereeing to workers we really don't **need**. During that week, "non-essential" workers were told to stay home. That accounted for about 90% of the federal workforce. Did you miss them?

By the time the shutdown rolled around, the Office Personnel Management cobbled together a new term for the people we really don't need to be working full-time for the federal government; "non-excepted". The term requires an explanation where non-essential doesn't. People were getting their noses out of joint about the old term. The perpetually offended said it was injurious to their self-esteem to be told they were unimportant. But most were worried the term demonstrated their true worth and that it might have a deleterious effect on their status among the New Aristocracy (federal employees).

[29] *Progress Made, but More Action Needed to Address Medicare Fraud, Waste, and Abuse* GAO-14-560T: Published: Apr 30, 2014. Publicly Released: Apr 30, 2014.

[30] *10--U. S. EPA Firearms Purchase - SIG Sauer P229* 22 Aug 2011

[31] *EPA Chief: 'Climate Deniers' Aren't Normal Human Beings* -Michael Bastasch – *Daily Caller*, 23 June 15

[32] People outside the beltway probably won't know this, but federal agencies are always trying to find ways to justify three-letter acronyms for their little empires. The NATIONAL IMAGERY AND MAPPING AGENCY (NIMA) got a boost in

prestige when it became the National Geospatial Intelligence Agency (NGA). I remembering thinking that very thing when driving by their headquarters shortly after the change; "Well, they're moving up in the world. "

33 LPMaryland.org, Madison quoted, 27 August 2014

34 *FAIL: US HAS WASTED $154 BILLION ON 'RENEWABLE ENERGY',* Breitbart. com, 5 December 2013. Pay particular attention to the kickbacks and sleazy politics involved.

Ch. 8

35 *MULTIPLE EMPLOYMENT AND TRAINING PROGRAMS **Providing Information on Collocating Services and Consolidating Administrative Structures Could Promote Efficiencies,*** GAO 11-92 January 2011

Ch. 9

36 *CORRECTIONS TO THE MANN et. al. al. al. (1998) PROXY DATA BASE AND NORTHERN HEMISPHERIC AVERAGE TEMPERATURE SERIES* Stephen McIntyre 512-120 Adelaide St. West, Toronto, Ontario Canada M5H 1T1; Ross McKitrick, Department of Economics, University

of Guelph, Guelph Ontario Canada N1G2W1 **Yeah, I actually do read this stuff. I need a life!**

[37] It is worth noting that hundreds of stations used to collect data now used to support man-made climate change alarmism are located in these very cities, often where development has surrounded the once-lonely stations. These are actually just boxes with sensors in them. They have been found next to steam plants, in newer, steaming hot parking lots and near large AC exhausts. And they have skewed the data wildly. *Distorted data? Feds close 600 weather stations amid criticism they're situated to report warming,* Maxim Lott, 13 August 2013, *FoxNews. com/science*

[38] Inside of a week, Martin O'Malley marked himself as one of the stupidest people ever to run for President. This is quite a challenge since he has Gore, Biden and Mondale for company. First, O'Malley apologized for saying that all lives matter as opposed to saying that only black lives matter. Then he blamed the rise of ISIS on GW/CC. *U. S. military bases eyed as 'green job' incubators* by Aaron Klein, WMD.com, 21 July 2015 and *James Woods rips into '100%*

numbskull' Martin O'Malley by Cheryl Chumley, WMD.com, 20 July 2015 Little tip for voters: Both Emperor Obama and Empress Rodham have both said that GW/CC is a major threat to national security. Anyone who says these things should not get to play a President in a sitcom much less be elected President.

Ch. 10

[39] The three biggest reasons for high healthcare costs are defensive medicine and fear of lawsuits, compliance costs foisted on the industry by bloated government, and the knowledge that the medical profession knows that the government/insurance company MUST provide payment. This last point is important. If a doctor is in the stable of several insurance companies, and possibly Medicare and Medicaid, they know the money is coming. So they will charge up to the maximum limit for everything. They don't have to compete for that dollar.

[40] We will discuss this in my chapter on taxes.

Ch. 12

[41] White House: It's A Good Thing That Obamacare Will Drive 2. 5 Million Americans Out Of The Workforce, Avik Roy, Forbes.com, 2 Feb

2014

Ch. 13

[42] There may be a waiver for this rule where Lithuanians are concerned. I swear they have their own mafia. I once watched a group of Lithuanians rearrange the cups and saucers in an antiques store and then run away giggling - after complimenting the proprietor on the décor, of course. Such cruelty! How did we ever come to this?

Ch.14

[43] *EPA chief says climate change deniers not 'normal'* By JOHN SICILIANO, National Examiner

[44] One reason for that may be the autoerotic thrill many of them get at seeing the US put at a disadvantage.

Ch. 15

[45] *Winston Churchill knew the value of our liberty* by Trevor Phillips, the Telegraph, 9 December 2008

[46] These are the first words concerning our data at https://nsa.gov1.info/data/. They were also words attributed to the National Socialists and

Communists in the last century when they would investigate citizens. I am sure Putin's goons still say it. What honest people **should fear** is that their government would actually put that on a website without a blush of irony!

[47] What a nasty rope of sausage this was! It amended the Electronic Communications Privacy Act - Computer Fraud and Abuse Act – Family Educational Rights and Privacy Act Privacy Act – Money Laundering Control Act – Bank Secrecy Act – Right to Financial Privacy Act – Immigration and Nationality Act – Fair Credit Reporting Act – Victims of Crime Act of 1984 – Telemarketing and Consumer Fraud and Abuse Prevention Act. It included some 118 other amendments.

[48] Red Team agents use disguises, ingenuity to expose TSA vulnerabilities, by Brian Bennett, LA Times, 2 June 2015. Note the insert in the article explaining that the people who got weapons past the goons at the gate were not "Red Team experts" but office weenies. But the original story and more importantly the big headline stands. *See? We can kind of tell the truth and protect Jeh Johnson and the emperor at the same time.*

[49] **FBI Knew al-Qaeda Pilots Training in U. S.** Agency Knew of Flight Training Before 9/11, Moussaoui Jury Told, By *Timothy Dwyer and*

William Branigin
Washington Post Staff Writers, Tuesday, March 7, 2006

[50] Trump has made half-baked comments along these lines, but he is not a serious candidate, as of 20 July. He's a real estate mogul and TV clown who believes some of the press accounts about himself. It remains to be seen if he will get serious.

Ch. 16

[51] The new and improved term for wars that don't need to be fought or are fought stupidly is *asymmetrical warfare.* That means one side is smaller and different than the other, so the dominant one has to half fight or it wouldn't be sporting. The remainder of the effort is devoted to the winning of hearts and minds.
[52] Korea only ran about 3 years. But they did a good job of clearing the warehouses of WWII surplus while losing 54,000 young Americans.

Ch. 17

[53] *No, Reagan Did Not Author the Republican's 11th Commandment* By KITTY BENNETT, New York Times blog, The Caucus 11 December 2011.

[54] I will state for the record that I personally like

Bush. I used to think we elected the wrong one last time. But time has shown Bush to be a Democrat statist – lite. If he goes up against Clinton, I fear the electorate will look at their choice and think well if it is a statist Democrat or a pale imitation of a statist Democrat, I'll take BJ Bill's wife. We need a candidate as capable of delivering rhetorical body blows at the Democrat as taking them. So far, that ain't Jeb.

55 *The Story Mike Huckabee Dreads*, Byron York, *National Review,* December 5, 2007. Also Google Huckabee on Social Security. He has chided candidates who acknowledge that without drastic changes, SSI will cease to exist or break the budget – SOON!

Ch. 18

56 Okay. I was joking! I know there are actually seven people who don't like the Philadelphia Eagles. They're funny looking and poorly educated. They even spread a nasty rumor that Eagles fans threw snowballs at Santa Claus. Piffle!

57 This followed a quintessentially Leahy attack on Cheney earlier that day. The attack was venomous and, as usual, untrue. Speaking form the well of the Senate, lawmakers often are protected in their speech, no matter how egregious (remember Harry Reid lying about

Romney's taxes) from civil consequences. What Leahy didn't appreciate was, unlike him, Cheney is prickly about speaking the truth. To this day Cheney considers his greeting appropriate and is rather proud of it.

[58] Does the reader understand the stupidity of our present method of law making? I just used the phrase, "Republicans approached the White House" in the context of writing a budget. This is a constitutional circus. The Congress is required to send the White House a budget and there it is vetoed or signed. They are not supposed to waste the taxpayers' money and time "negotiating" away their jobs until the last minute, which in this case guarantees a shutdown atmosphere. This is just another example of an overly powerful executive and a morally bankrupt Congress.

Ch. 19

[59] Both quotes: *The 25 Best Quotes About Liberals* by John Hawkins, Townhall.com | Nov 23, 2010

[60] For the record I am against abortion on demand and certainly don't want to fund it. This is not a religious position. I am non-religious. I view abortions of convenience as a barbaric abrogation of responsibility. Rape, incest, life of the mother? Of course. It would help if there

were more men in this country to share the burden. Sadly we have too many lame, limp little boys.

Ch. 20

[61] I have a real problem with this. Absentee ballots for insurmountable extenuating circumstances are one thing. But weeks of voting, mail-in ballots for anyone who wants one, and no paper ballots provide too much opportunity for chicanery.

[62] Joe Bergeron, Full Metal Roofing, Inc.